GOD'S
GAME
PLAN

Strategies for
Abundant Living

AUBREY JOHNSON

GOD'S

GAME
PLAN

Strategies for
Abundant Living

AUBREY JOHNSON

GOSPEL
ADVOCATE
A TRUSTED NAME SINCE 1855

Also by Aubrey Johnson

The Barnabas Factor

Love More, Sin Less

Renewing Your Spiritual Life

The Seed Principle

Spiritual Patriots

Published by Gospel Advocate Co.
1006 Elm Hill Pike, Nashville, TN 37210
www.gospeladvocate.com

ISBN: 978-0-89225-646-4

Dedication

To Denny Loyd,
for his encouragement
and inspiring life of service to Christ
(educator, evangelist, elder, editor, encourager).

Acknowledgments

Special thanks to six friends
who blessed me with their feedback:

Tim Alsup

Stan Butt

Craig Evans

Matt Hearn

Amanzo Jones

David Shannon

Table of Contents

About
This Book

**"It's not the will to win, but the will to prepare
to win that makes the difference."**
– Paul "Bear" Bryant, Coach, Alabama Crimson Tide

Whether you were a player, fan, cheerleader or band member, you probably have pleasant memories of pep rallies and game nights that will last your lifetime. Drawing on these and other football experiences, this book lays out God's game plan for successful living.

In John 10:10, Jesus announced: "I have come that [you] may have life, and that [you] may have it more abundantly." Do you want a new start in life? Would you like to make the most of your days on earth? This book will show you how. A great life consists of positive relationships, personal growth and a profound contribution to the lives of those around you. By living a life of mastery and ministry, you will flourish as never before.

Using a football field analogy, this book identifies 10 targets of Christian growth that serve as milestones for advancing to spiritual maturity (see "The Spiritual Growth Chart" on page 10). The near end of the field stands for increasing self-mastery. The far end signifies growth in ministry. The goal lines on both ends are marked by grace, which covers the expanse of the field. It is through grace that you are saved from your past sins when you obey the gospel. It is through grace that you partake of heaven's joy following the judgment.

THE
SPIRITUAL GROWTH
CHART

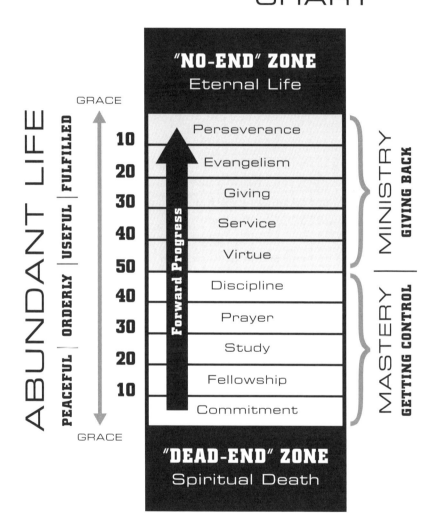

Areas of growth are not
necessarily sequential.

Chapter Breakdown

Choose Your Team: Live Decisively

Chapters 1 and 2 explain how the "game" of life works and why it is crucial to play for God's team.

This section contains an "Initial Growth Assessment" (see page 22) to help you determine the growth areas you need to work on most. Then, in the back of the book are three "Growth Plan" sheets to help you take effective action in the three areas of your life you most need to improve.

Regular Season: Live Abundantly

The next 10 chapters present 10 growth strategies for living the abundant life.

- **Mastery (Getting Control):** Chapters 3 through 7 describe how you can take back control of your life through commitment, fellowship, Bible study, prayer and discipline.
- **Ministry (Giving Back):** After gaining control, there comes a time to give back in gratitude for the blessings you have received. Chapters 8 through 12 explain how you move from mastery to ministry through growth in virtue, service, giving, evangelism and perseverance.

Postseason: Live Eternally

The final chapter looks ahead to life's postseason to inspire a longing for heaven.

God wants to help you live decisively, abundantly and eternally. His Word is the ultimate playbook for positive living. Make Him your coach, and start living victoriously today.

> "But thanks be to God, who gives us the victory through our Lord Jesus Christ"
> (1 Corinthians 15:57).

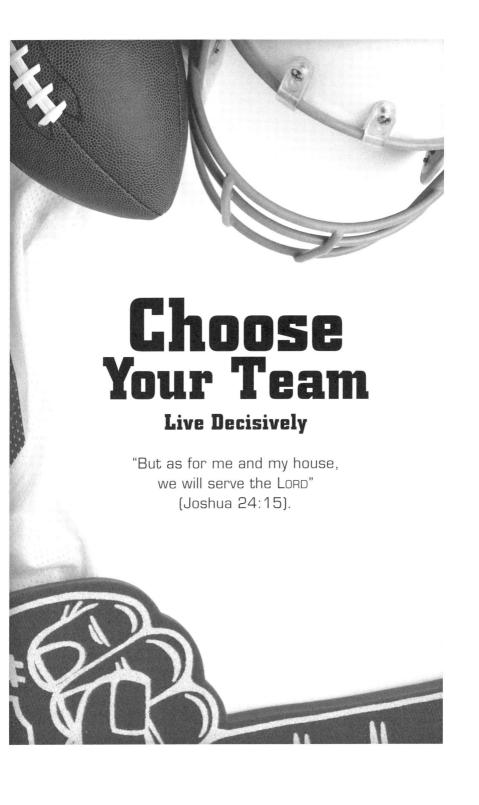

Choose Your Team

Live Decisively

"But as for me and my house,
we will serve the LORD"
(Joshua 24:15).

The
Game of Life

"Do you know what my favorite part of the game is? The opportunity to play."
– Mike Singletary, Linebacker, Chicago Bears

Jesus often taught His followers by comparing heavenly truths with earthly experiences. In American culture, few things are as familiar and popular as sports. In the fall, football reigns as the king of athletic competition. Following Jesus' example, this book uses football (an earthly experience) to illustrate the importance of spiritual growth and to mark a clear path for attaining spiritual maturity.

Christ called this lifelong growth process "abundant life." Simply put, it is life as God intended, full and overflowing with spiritual blessings. Making this quality of life accessible to you was Jesus' reason for coming to earth. In John 10:10, He declared, "I have come that [you] may have life, and that [you] may have it more abundantly." The key to enjoying an abundant life is following Jesus' teaching and example. By becoming a better person, you experience a more rewarding life. But never forget that the joy is in the journey.

The Goal of Life

The ultimate goal of football is not to score the most points or win the most games (although some have lost sight of this fact).

It is more than a pastime or business, and it does more than entertain crowds and raise revenue for investors and institutions. The higher purpose of football is to teach lessons about the game of life. Participants learn the value of teamwork and hard work. They discover the importance of preparation and execution. Football develops a player's ability to endure in the face of obstacles and exhaustion. It teaches resilience in the face of defeat and discouragement.

Some fans only see the scoreboard, but the coach and parents see much more: They see the player. They know that games and seasons come and go, but life continues. They understand that today's circumstances give way to tomorrow's opportunities and that developing character is far more important than statistics or trophies.

If football is about growth gained rather than yards gained, it makes you wonder: What is God up to as I take my place on the field of life? Does He have a purpose for me? Can I know His plan for my life? How does He measure success? Am I moving forward or slipping back? This study was designed to answer these questions.

God's Game Plan for Abundant Living

Spiritual growth is the secret to abundant life. It begins with salvation from your past sins and continues with sanctification or growth in Christlikeness (Galatians 2:20; Ephesians 4:13). The key to forgiveness and spiritual growth is to follow God's game plan in the Bible. The New Testament reveals 10 growth strategies to help you move forward in life. They are hash marks for a holy life.

In football, yard markers help players measure their progress. The first-down marker shows a ball carrier exactly where he needs to be. As a result, he stretches to reach beyond it. Without field markings, it would be hard for a player to gauge his progress or enjoy the thrill of success.

For the Christian, Satan is your opponent; he hopes to stop your progress in the faith. Life is the field of play, and continual growth (abundant life) is the goal. God is your coach; He challenges you to be your best. The church is your team to support you in reaching your spiritual potential. The Bible is God's game plan for life, and your daily choices make up the series of downs. Think of the football itself as your relationship with God stitched together with faith, hope and love. With every situation you encounter, you must keep your hold on these three to move forward. When you lose your grip, you go on defense until you regain control. To keep from fumbling, you must control your thoughts, words and deeds.

These analogies are not perfect, but if they help you get a better feel for the Christian life, they have served their purpose. Figurative analogies draw out similarities between things that are different in fundamental ways. For example, Christians must become like children to enter the kingdom of heaven (Matthew 18:3), but there are some ways you should not be childlike. Likewise, life is more than a game, and God is more than a coach; so do not press these analogies too far. Within proper limits, however, they are useful illustrations of valuable spiritual truths. With this in mind, it is time to take the field.

When you become a Christian, you enter the arena of faith, and your struggle against sin begins in earnest. God told Cain: "Sin lies at the door. And its desire is for you, but you should rule over it" (Genesis 4:7). The New American Standard Bible says, "You must master it." Sin interferes with God's master plan for your life. To reach your potential, you must face your sins and overcome them through faith in Christ (1 John 5:4). Satan will never forfeit the game and walk away, but he can be beaten (4:4). When you trust and obey God, the devil loses ground.

Ease or Honor?

Jesus never promised His people a trouble-free life. In fact, Scripture is filled with assurances that life will not be easy. Job said, "Man who is born of woman is few of days and full of trouble" (Job 14:1). Paul preached that it is through "many tribulations" you enter the kingdom of God (Acts 14:22) and that all who "live godly in Christ Jesus will suffer persecution"

(2 Timothy 3:12). Jesus said, "Sufficient for the day is its own trouble" (Matthew 6:34). Prophets were martyred, John the Baptist was beheaded, Paul suffered a thorn in the flesh, and God's Son was crucified.

The fact is you will get sick. People you love will die. You are subject to accidents, recessions, swine flu, and eventually, you will die. Before that day comes, you will get your heart broken more times than you want to remember. However, God promises to provide what you need to overcome adversity and triumph over it gloriously (Romans 8:37). The abundant life is not an easy life, an affluent life, or a trouble-free life. It is a life of honor, courage, love and usefulness in the face of hardship and heartache.

The Abundant Life

Abundant living occurs when you have the confidence and capacity to meet life's demands. Paul said, "I can do all things through Christ who strengthens me" (Philippians 4:13). "All things" does not refer to technical knowledge or skills. You cannot perform surgery or play the violin the moment you are baptized, but you are on a path to increased emotional and relational stability. You can get along better with others thanks to the fruit of the Spirit. You can set and reach meaningful goals because you understand the law of sowing and reaping. You can make the most of your God-given potential because faith frees you from fear, pride and worry. Jesus empowers you to live a peaceful, joyful, fruitful life.

You are able to meet life's demands because a Christian mindset allows you not only to cope but to flourish. Whatever life throws at you, you know you can handle it. In Philippians, Paul was talking about the spiritual strength Christ affords you to fully engage life (2 Timothy 1:7). To live abundantly is to constantly learn, adjust and grow to become the best possible you. The more you trust and obey Jesus, the holier and better you become. Consider these five marks of abundant living.

1. Faithfulness

The key to success is your faithfulness to God's Word (Ezra 7:9-10). Disobedience causes dysfunction and dissatisfaction. Four things are necessary to live faithfully. You must

- Immerse yourself in Christ's teaching (Colossians 3:16-17).
- Trust it is best for producing the life you want (Romans 12:2).
- Obey His commands to enjoy His blessings (James 1:22).
- Persevere in your commitment to do His will (2 Timothy 4:7).

2. Functionality

A functional life has a balance, flow and usefulness that results from an awakened spirit. When this occurs, you flourish spiritually, and a constant stream of blessings comes your way.

- **Physical Blessings:** Warnings against destructive behaviors like adultery, drunkenness and gluttony protect your body from disease and degeneration. The Bible also stresses the connection between rest and spiritual wellness.
- **Mental Blessings:** As a believer, you view the world and its circumstances with a different perspective than nonbelievers. (Philippians 4:8). Faith rids your life of pointless worry, needless fear and other kinds of useless thinking.
- **Emotional Blessings**: Love and goodwill strengthen your spirit and stabilize your relationships. Strong faith is the remedy for deep despair. Christians are resilient because of the power of hope.

3. Fruitfulness

The word "fruitful" refers to the beneficial results of growth in the Lord. It speaks of spiritual success and prosperity (Joshua 1:8). By abiding in Christ, you become more and achieve more (Ephesians 3:20). The fruit of the Spirit makes you more Christlike and helps you to thrive in your endeavors (Galatians 5:22-23; 2 Peter 3:18).

4. Fulfillment

Christianity is a gratifying life overflowing with joy and thanksgiving (1 Thessalonians 5:16-18). The gospel regulates human emotions to produce more peace and less pain (2 Corinthians 7:10). No one will awaken in eternity and be disappointed for trusting Jesus (Romans 5:5). Although you will fall short of perfection, forgiveness and renewal are available whenever you repent. Jesus fills your soul's longings so perfectly that you will never hunger or thirst for more than He has to offer (John 6:35).

5. Fearlessness

Courage is necessary to live well and enjoy God's blessings. You will be tempted to doubt what God says and pressured to compromise His teachings. Satan uses fear of rejection, financial loss, physical harm and death to test your conviction. The answer to fear is more faith and more love (Matthew 8:26; 1 John 4:18). Godly fear is a good thing (Proverbs 9:10), but spiritual timidity is destructive (2 Timothy 1:7). "Be strong in the Lord and in the power of His might" (Ephesians 6:10).

Live Abundantly

Abundant living is not an impossible dream. For faithful Christians, it is an everyday reality. Equipped with faith, they face problems rather than hide from them. Outfitted with courage, they embrace responsibilities rather than run from them. Simply put, an abundant life is a God-honoring life. As you grow, He is glorified. When you are blessed, He is magnified. Why? Your growth and blessings are derived from faith in His Son and obedience to His Word. Your spiritual health and well-being are a testimony to His love and wisdom. He is good and gracious. Therefore, to praise Him and serve Him is to live a life worth living. Imagine if people took their spiritual lives as seriously as some fans take football. What a wonderful world it would be.

Questions

1. What was Jesus' most memorable teaching method?

2. What familiar scenes did Jesus use to illustrate spiritual truths?

3. What should Christians do with problems?

4. What is the higher purpose of football (athletics)?

5. Who is the Christian's coach?

6. What is the Christian's team?

7. What is the Christian's playbook?

8. What is the Christian's goal?

9. Who is the Christian's opponent?

10. What are five marks of an abundant life? (Each begins with the letter "f.")

For Discussion

1. How is life similar to football? How is it different?

2. Are most Christians as devoted to their spiritual lives as football fans are devoted to football? Why, or why not?

3. If you are a Christian, how has knowing Christ made your life more abundant?

Play of the Day

Memorize the 10 growth areas from "The Spiritual Growth Chart" (on page 10). Commit yourself to reciting the list every day for the duration of this study. By doing this, you will enhance your study and guarantee it will stay with you long after you are done.

Also, complete the "Initial Growth Assessment" on page 22. This will help you determine what growth areas you specifically need to work on before you begin reading the chapters about each of them. Take your time with the assessment, and be honest with yourself so you can start down the road to abundant living.

Initial Growth Assessment

**Rank yourself from 1 to 10 in the areas
of growth below, as shown on
"The Spiritual Growth Chart" on page 10.**

(10 = high, 1 = low)

Perseverance _____   Discipline _____

Evangelism _____   Prayer _____

Giving _____   Study _____

Service _____   Fellowship _____

Virtue _____   Commitment _____

What are your top three areas of growth?

1 _____

2 _____

3 _____

What are your bottom three areas of growth?

1 _____

2 _____

3 _____

As you read the chapters pertaining to your bottom three areas
of growth, use the "Growth Plan" sheets provided in the back of
the book to plan ways to improve in each of these areas.

The
Perfect Coach

**"Coaching is a profession of love.
You can't coach people unless you love them."**
– Eddie Robinson, Coach, Grambling State Tigers

W ant to start an argument? Ask a football fan who is the greatest football coach of all time. Many factors go into defining a great coach, and people weigh them differently. When it comes to high school football, Mom's idea of a good coach may be different from a fan's.

So what makes a coach good or bad? If he loses all his games but graduates all his players, you might say he is a good person but not a good coach. If he wins all his games but does not prepare his players for life, he may seem like a good coach, but really isn't. He may be a good recruiter, strategist and motivator, but not a good coach. A bad human being will never be an exceptional coach. Great coaches have victories on and off the field.

What Is a Coach?

The word "coach" came from horse-drawn carriages used to transport people to their destinations. A person who assists others in reaching their goals is a kind of coach. For example, teachers and tutors convey students through their examinations toward graduation. Corporate and life coaches help clients achieve success by reaching personal and professional objectives. Sports coaches transport players through demanding seasons and stages of growth: from rookie to veteran.

In football, a head coach is the person accountable for assembling, training and directing his team. He is responsible for the larger issues confronting an athletic organization. He establishes policy, sets direction and coordinates group effort. In the Christian faith, there are many similarities between God and a head coach.

Meet the Coach

God has assembled an outstanding coaching staff to bring out the best in His followers. The elders in a local church are His assistant coaches (1 Peter 5:1-4). Teachers and preachers are fitness specialists who supply spiritual nutrition and strength exercises (2 Timothy 4:2). Parents are superb trainers (Proverbs 22:6; Ephesians 6:4). Loving brethren are his medical staff to heal spiritual injuries (Galatians 6:1-2).

God calls His team into being through the preaching of the gospel. Every Christian is a recruiter, and church buildings are His spiritual training facilities. When you walk out of the auditorium, you are stepping onto the playing field of life. That does not discount what takes place in worship, but assembly times prepare saints for what follows. Those who believe they have fulfilled their religious obligations by attending a service are like football players who practice hard but never show up for the game.

Qualities of a Great Coach

One question remains to be answered: Is God qualified to fill this role in your life? Consider God's qualifications for leading you to a more abundant life. A great coach is …

Smart

> "'For My thoughts are not your thoughts, nor are your ways My ways,' says the LORD. 'For as the heavens are higher than the earth, so are My ways higher than your ways'" (Isaiah 55:8-9).

A winning coach must be mentally sharp. He understands the game of football and human nature. God is not merely astute. He is all-knowing. He sees far into the future and deep into the heart. Satan is a cunning adversary, but God's wisdom puts Him in a class all by Himself.

Engaged

> "O LORD, You have searched me
> and known me. You know my sitting down
> and my rising up; You understand my thought
> afar off. You comprehend my path and my lying
> down, and are acquainted with all my ways. For
> there is not a word on my tongue, but behold, O
> LORD, You know it altogether" (Psalm 139:1-4).

Some coaches are preoccupied with their own press or personal issues. The heavenly Father is focused on you. Because God is ever-present, He is never distracted or absentminded. His ears are open to your prayers, and His heart is open to your cares.

Experienced

> "Before the mountains were brought forth,
> or ever You had formed the earth
> and the world, even from everlasting
> to everlasting, You are God" (Psalm 90:2).

The Lord is eternal. In other words, He has spent time in the trenches. He is not a novice, wet behind the ears. Coaches who are green and gullible are ill-prepared to compete. God knows the wiles of the devil and is not susceptible to his trick plays.

Energetic

> "And what is the exceeding greatness of His power toward us who believe, according to the working of His mighty power?" (Ephesians 1:19).

God is not lazy or passive. He creates, redeems and transforms while overseeing every detail of the universe. His remarkable activity stirs Christians to demand more of themselves by pressing toward the mark of the high calling of God in Christ Jesus (Philippians 3:14).

Composed

> "He only is my rock and my salvation; He is my defense, I shall not be moved" (Psalm 62:6).

When it looks like momentum has shifted to your adversary, it is crucial to keep your head in the game. No matter the circumstance, God does not fret or fall apart. Certain of victory, He does not fear what Satan or man can do. Confidence and composure are marks of true greatness.

Caring

> "Cast your burden on the LORD, and He shall sustain you; He shall never permit the righteous to be moved" (Psalm 55:22).

A superior coach is a considerate person. He wants to develop his players' character as well as their stamina. Therefore, he takes a personal interest in each athlete. He is not distant or aloof. He knows their names, personalities, strengths and weaknesses. George Halas, Chicago Bears coach, commented: "What makes a good coach? Complete dedication." Because He loves you, God is completely dedicated to helping you live a victorious life.

Honorable

> "Holy, holy, holy is the LORD of hosts; the whole earth is full of His glory!" (Isaiah 6:3).

If character is the mark of a complete coach, then God is truly sublime. Trust is the foundation of lasting influence. God's holiness makes Him credible, reliable and inspirational. He keeps His word at all times (Joshua 21:45; 23:14). Coaches who lack character are unfinished leaders. They know x's and o's but cannot lift people's souls.

Instructive

> "All Scripture is given by inspiration of God, and is profitable for doctrine, for reproof, for correction, for instruction in righteousness, that the man of God may be complete, thoroughly equipped for every good work" (2 Timothy 3:16-17).

Great coaches are exceptional teachers. They impart information that enables athletes to succeed in their roles. In Jesus' church, God put a premium on spiritual instruction and continual learning (1 Timothy 3:15). Education lies at the core of God's system, and His knowledge of the game of life is unsurpassed.

Challenging

> "Every branch that bears fruit He prunes, that it may bear more fruit" (John 15:2).

God specializes in helping Christians reach beyond their present level of spiritual growth and service. He knows when you need a pat on the back or a push in the right direction. While self-acceptance is essential for mental health, self-satisfaction can destroy your desire to improve. God loves you as you are, but He never stops challenging you to be your very best. He calls you to leave your comfort zone so you can fulfill your untapped potential.

Encouraging

> "Blessed be the God and Father of our Lord Jesus Christ, the Father of mercies and God of all comfort, who comforts us in all our tribulation, that we may be able to comfort those who are in any trouble, with the comfort with which we ourselves are comforted by God" (2 Corinthians 1:3-4).

Football is psychological as well as physical. In addition to fit bodies, players need emotional fitness to play their best. That is why God is the perfect coach. He knows that sustained effort comes from a steady supply of encouragement.

Choose Your Team

In sports and faith, choosing your team is a big decision. God and Satan are heavily recruiting you, but the final choice is yours. A wise person asks two things before making a commitment: Which coach truly cares for me, and which one can I trust to help me? Why choose the devil's empty boasts when God has a proven record (1 Kings 8:56)? Take a minute to review God's résumé. Ask yourself, who else would I possibly want as my life coach?

Yet no matter how good the coach is, each player must accept responsibility for his performance on the field. The key to greater success is more discipline. My friend Chris Parker tells a story that illustrates this point. After pulling into a restaurant parking lot, his preschool son, Jackson, discovered a pile of rocks perfect for tossing. Chris told him not to throw the rocks because he might accidentally hit a car or injure someone. Sensing how great the temptation was, he repeated the warning with this added admonition: "You need to use your self-control." Chris could tell his son was engaged in an epic struggle, so he left him alone with his decision. A few minutes later, a delighted

Jackson came running up, exclaiming: "Dad, Dad, guess what! I self-controlled myself!" Whether you are 4 or 44, it is a wonderful thing to discover you can exercise control over your life.

Abundant life begins with the decision to play for God's team, but ultimate victory is not possible without spiritual discipline. Your heavenly Coach can draw up perfect plays, put them in a book for you, and remind you to do your homework, but He cannot study and practice for you. You must have the desire and discipline to prepare yourself for the challenges of life. The Bible reveals God's game plan for spiritual growth, but what you do with that information is up to you. The strategies work flawlessly but you must apply them faithfully. Isn't it time to self-control yourself?

Pure Joy

There is only one perfect Coach, and it is pure joy to play on His team. His win/loss record is unsurpassed, and when the last buzzer (trumpet) sounds, there is no doubt who will come out on top. In the end, those who side with Him will enjoy the greatest victory in history. You will have missteps along the way, but He will get you through. Following Christ will not be a walk in the park, but it will be worth every sacrifice. So are you ready to commit?

Questions

1. How is God like a smart coach?

2. How is God like an engaged coach?

3. How is God like an experienced coach?

4. How is God like an energetic coach?

5. How is God like a composed coach?

6. How is God like a caring coach?

7. How is God like an honorable coach?

8. How is God like an instructive coach?

  9. How is God like a challenging coach?

  10. How is God like an encouraging coach?

For Discussion

  1. What makes an exceptional coach?

  2. How is God like a coach? How is He different?

  3. Why would anyone choose to play for Satan's team?

Play of the Day

Take a piece of paper, and divide it in half. At the top of the left column, write "God," and at the top of the right column, write "Satan." Now list the pros and cons of playing for each team. After you finish, compare the two lists, and make a commitment. It is time to get off the fence.

Regular Season

Live Abundantly

"I have come that they may have life, and that they may have it more abundantly" (John 10:10).

Mastery

Growth Strategies 1-5: Getting Control

**"Winning isn't getting ahead of others.
It is getting ahead of yourself."**
– Roger Staubach, Quarterback, Dallas Cowboys

The hardest part of football is not facing your opponent but facing the truth about yourself. Your mind and body are weak and resist the intense preparation that top performance demands. The coach's job is to push you beyond your comfort zone to reach your potential. Mentally and physically, you must become a new person to meet the challenges of the game. Physical fitness and mental toughness are honed one drill and one down at a time. A new person emerges as toned muscles and true grit replace the flabby, weak-willed walk-on who started the season.

Although people come to Christ in various states of readiness, their beginning is similar to the conditioning football players go through to prepare for a grueling season. Gaining self-mastery is the key to success. In the next five chapters, you will learn five growth strategies for retaking control of your spiritual life. Through commitment, fellowship, Bible study, prayer and discipline, you will develop the spiritual strength it takes to succeed in the game of life. Spiritual living begins with conquering your own will and bringing it into the service of Christ.

Are you ready to leave a life of ease in order to begin a life of dedication? Then turn the page, and step onto the field where greatness is born. The Coach has been waiting for you.

Growth Strategy #1
Commitment

"No one has ever drowned in sweat."
– Lou Holtz, Coach, Notre Dame

To win at football, you must take your place on the field. No one ever won a game from the bleachers or the sideline or by cowering in his own end zone. The same is true of life. There comes a time to stand up and be counted or slink into the shadows of conformity. Those who yield to fear or lust are bullied by the world around them. They lack the courage to be their true and best selves. Instead, they swap their potential for momentary peace or pleasure. To fit in or feel good, they sacrifice the greatness of which they are capable.

But those who step boldly onto the playing field of faith declare that their time on earth will count no matter the cost. They are ready to reveal God's glory to a world in darkness. They refuse to back down in the face of trial or temptation. Come what may, they will honor the One who made them for holiness and heaven.

The Essence of a Commitment

To become a Christian, then, is to make a commitment. To make a commitment is to obligate yourself. When you make a commitment, you agree to do something. You undertake what you promised, and you see it through to completion. Therefore, the word "commitment" implies a guarantee. It is a pledge backed up by your personal honor.

During your lifetime, you will make many commitments. In school, you commit to extracurricular activities such as sports, band and chorus. Military service involves a multi-year commitment to serve your country. A marriage vow is a solemn commitment to love your spouse until death. However, the most important commitment you can make is to Jesus. When you become a Christian, you obligate yourself to follow His teaching (John 8:31; 14:15). You make Him the Lord of your life and base every decision on pleasing Him (2 Timothy 2:4).

Achieving greatness in life requires making and keeping commitments. Those who walk away from their promises damage themselves. Momentary relief comes at the expense of character and credibility. Commitments summon you to grow. Compromise shrivels your soul.

It is not wrong to abandon mistaken beliefs or self-defeating behaviors. Holding stubbornly to something that diminishes you is not honor but pride. It is one thing to keep a difficult commitment. It is another thing to keep a destructive one.

Walking away from your commitment to Christ is never the right choice. Peter said that abandoning Christ and returning to a life of worldliness is like a dog returning to its vomit (2 Peter 2:22). If it made you sick the first time, why would you want a second helping? For those who seek spiritual nourishment, Christ is "the bread of life" (John 6:35).

God's Commitment to You

The Bible is a book about commitment. The best example of commitment is God's dedication to His people. The Lord promised, "I will never leave, nor forsake you" (Hebrews 13:5). Paul boasted that nothing can "separate us from the love of God which is in Christ Jesus our Lord" (Romans 8:38-39). David likened the Lord to a caring shepherd whose devotion is seen in the way He tends His flock (Psalm 23:1). When you are hungry, tired, sick or afraid, He is there to meet your needs and comfort your heart.

Jesus' Commitment to You

Jesus called Himself "the good shepherd" (John 10:11). The word "good" refers to His genuine concern for His followers and the reliable care He provides them. Most people pursue their personal, narrow interests, but Jesus declared, "I have come that they may have life, and that they may have it more abundantly" (v. 10).

The thing that differentiates a good shepherd from a hireling is his level of dedication. When a single sheep is missing, a good shepherd sets out to recover it (Luke 15:3-7). He knows the names of his sheep, watches over them tirelessly, and will not abandon them when attacked. "The good shepherd gives His life for the sheep" (John 10:11). No greater commitment is possible.

Jesus is caring and courageous like a shephcrd, but He is also as unshakable as a rock. According to Matthew 7:24-27, His words provide the spiritual groundwork needed to weather life's storms. Your success in life is conditioned on your commitment to Christ. It is the foundation of everything.

Why should you commit to Christ? Because He is worthy of your complete confidence. His trustworthiness is evident in everything He has done for you:

- He gave up heaven for you (2 Corinthians 8:9).
- He left an example for you (1 Peter 2:21).
- He defeated death for you (Hebrews 2:14-15).
- He intercedes for you (Hebrews 7:25; 1 John 2:1).
- He is coming back for you (John 14:1-3).

How to Commit to Christ

God's Word reveals five things people do to begin a life of devotion to Christ.

1. Hear

Commitment to Christ begins with hearing His story and understanding His purpose. Jesus is God's Son, and He came to rescue lost souls from the misery of sin. Through His death on the cross, He offers forgiveness and the hope of heaven to those who follow Him.

2. Believe

Deep commitment is a consequence of deep faith. In other words, the strength of a belief determines the firmness of your commitment. The word "conviction" describes this kind of strong persuasion. Peter was expressing a heartfelt conviction when he proclaimed that Jesus was "the Christ, the Son of the living God" (Matthew 16:16). Strong belief produces a level of dedication that can survive life's ups and downs.

3. Repent

Jesus demands that His followers renounce sinfulness and selfishness. They must turn their hearts from worldliness to spiritual growth and service. This mental shift sets a Christian apart. The goal of life becomes pleasing God rather than self. Through holiness and helpfulness, Christians glorify God and advance His kingdom.

4. Confess

Important commitments are strengthened by verbalizing them. Commissioned officers of the armed services take an oath of enlistment. Immigrants who want to become U.S. citizens take an oath of allegiance. At weddings, the bride and groom exchange vows to express their commitment to each other. They pledge undying devotion "in joy and in sorrow, in sickness and in health, in plenty and in want, so long as [they] both shall live."

If society recognizes the value of verbalizing important commitments, is it any surprise that commitment to Christ involves a baptismal confession? In this case, the declaration involves an expression of certainty that Jesus is the Christ, the Son of the living God (Luke 1:3-4; Acts 8:36-38).

5. Be Baptized

According to the New Testament, submitting to baptism is the first thing you do once you decide to give your life to Jesus. Baptism visibly demonstrates commitment to Christ. By reenacting His death, burial and resurrection, you openly claim Him as your Savior and Lord. In addition, you are pledging to put away your old selfish ways in order to begin a new life patterned after Him. Baptism drives a stake in the ground of your memory. It turns a mental commitment into a physical experience never to be forgotten.

Now It Is Your Turn

Your commitment to Christ is a unique and exclusive agreement. It binds you to love and serve Jesus above all others. It takes priority over family relations (Matthew 10:37) and worldly pursuits (2 Timothy 2:4). Yet commitment to Christ does not diminish your relationships or job performance. In fact, your marriage and career will never reach their full potential apart from devotion to Christ.

Frankly, you cannot have too much commitment to Christ. The more faithful you are, the more functional you are. Commitment to Christ makes your life more abundant rather than less. If you believe your faith is holding you back from fulfillment, there is a problem somewhere. Either you do not understand true happiness, or you have mistaken ideas about Christian devotion. Christian commitment is about becoming the best possible you. Obeying Jesus makes you a better parent, spouse, boss, employee, friend and neighbor. He alone provides the joy and peace you desire.

Those who think happiness is found by limiting their commitment to Christ are sadly mistaken. The Laodiceans' halfheartedness brought a stern rebuke from the Lord (Revelation 3:14-22). Half a commitment is no commitment at all. While everyone will fall short of perfection, there is a difference between those who struggle and those who settle. To be lukewarm is to let the fire of your enthusiasm go out. Indifference sets in, and you find yourself going through the motions without your former zeal. Passion pleases the Lord, but passiveness sickens Him. Genuine faith sets your soul aflame and burns like fire in your bones.

Imagine Peter and Paul trying to keep their faith within socially acceptable limits. When hauled before an angry Sanhedrin, how would a timid man have responded (Acts 4:19-20)? When stoned or shipwrecked, how would a spineless person have reacted (2 Corinthians 4:8-9)? Those who turned the world upside down with their preaching were not cowardly or casually committed. They were disciples, not dabblers.

Attempting to negotiate with Christ rather than surrendering to Him is a big mistake. Christian living is a blessing to be enjoyed, not a burden to be borne. It satisfies the deepest longings of your spirit, although it frustrates the desires of your flesh.

The real problem is not too much Jesus but too little Jesus. So how much Jesus do you want? The rich young ruler thought by letting go of Christ and holding onto his money, he would attain greater happiness. Instead, the instant he moved away from Christ, sorrow overtook him (Matthew 19:16-22; Luke 18:18-23). Your choice is no different. Restricting His influence will limit your joy and potential.

Commitment and Courage

Without courage, there can be no commitment because commitment always involves a cost. Courage is your willingness to pay that price of commitment. It is rare and admired because it does not come cheap.

Biblical examples of brave men and women can inspire courage, but hearing their stories cannot guarantee your courage. You must look within to find strength to face life's challenges. How will you respond under pressure, and how will you know the right choice? It will not be the easiest or the most popular one. Instead, it will be the most caring and constructive one. When the moment of decision arrives, look deep into your soul, which was created in God's image and filled with His teaching. You will find the answer there. The courageous choice is the most loving one.

Love is the basis of meaningful commitment. Because God is love, the more you adore Him, the more committed you are to a life of love. You cannot worship God "in spirit and truth" (John 4:24) and withhold love from your fellowman. It is simply impossible. John explained:

> If someone says, "I love God," and hates his brother, he is a liar; for he who does not love his brother whom he has seen, how can he love God whom he has not seen? And this commandment we have from him: that he who loves God must love his brother also. (1 John 4:20-21)

A commitment is something you keep; something your heart compels you to do. Jesus said, "If you love Me, keep My commandments" (John 14:15). This is a statement of fact as well as a command. When you love people as He instructed, you confirm your love for Him (15:12). Love and obedience are signs of spiritual health. They prove your devotion to Christ (13:35). That is why honoring your commitments is the starting point of a more abundant life. It requires you to grow spiritually, and growing more Christlike is the key to enjoying life at its best. Keep your commitments, and you keep your soul (Luke 21:19).

Questions

1. What are many people willing to swap their potential for?

2. Describe what is means to make a commitment.

3. How is a commitment like a guarantee?

4. How does walking away from a commitment damage you?

5. To what did Peter compare abandoning your commitment?

6. What is the best example of commitment?

7. What does being the "good" shepherd indicate about Jesus?

8. Name five things people do to become devoted disciples of Christ.

9. What quality is necessary to have commitment?

10. What is the supreme source of courage?

For Discussion

1. How docs breaking a commitment damage you?

2. How does keeping a difficult commitment benefit you?

3. Are there times when it makes sense to break a commitment?

4. How has your commitment to Christ been tested?

5. Where do you find strength to remain faithful?

Play of the Day

Practice making and keeping a commitment. Sometime today, make a promise to do a good deed for someone, and fulfill it before the week is out. Be sure to put a reminder where you cannot miss it, and make a mental note of the things that tempt you to break your commitment. Make every effort to follow through despite inconveniences, and observe how you feel after keeping your promise.

Growth Strategy #2
Fellowship

"If a team is to reach its potential, each player must be willing to subordinate his personal goals to the good of the team."
– Bud Wilkinson, Coach, Oklahoma Sooners

When teams are not winning, players are usually more concerned with their own press than group success. Good coaches know the key to victory is renewed focus on teamwork. Vince Lombardi, Green Bay Packers coach, said, "Individual commitment to a group effort – that is what makes a team work, a company work, a society work, a civilization work." It is also what makes a church work.

Moving from sports to spiritual matters, Paul used human anatomy to explain the value of teamwork in the church: "For as the body is one and has many members, but all the members of that one body, being many, are one body, so also is Christ" (1 Corinthians 12:12). Every Christian has unique abilities that contribute to the well-being of the group (vv. 15-19), and saints serve in various roles to accomplish the Lord's work (vv. 28-30). What makes the parts work in harmony is an abundance of love (12:31–13:13). Concern for others is essential to personal and congregational growth.

Troubles arise when pride and selfishness enter the picture. In a healthy church, everyone values the contributions of others (Philippians 2:3). Members look out for one another's interests, not just their own (v. 4). Churches filled with big egos have big problems. In the opera, a prima donna is the lead female singer. On teams, a prima donna is a vain person whose egotism disrupts the group. Whatever talent the person has is minimized by insensitivity and difficulty. The church functions best when you learn to put the group before yourself.

Right behind your commitment to Christ comes your commitment to His church. The church is God's dream team. It was conceived in His mind "before the foundation of the world" (Ephesians 1:3-4). The church exists to spread God's kingdom and improve people's lives. If 12 committed men could turn the world upside down with their message of faith, hope and love, just imagine what your congregation can do.

How to Commit to the Church

The church is a band of brothers fighting the good fight (Hebrews 2:11). They protect the once-delivered faith, defend the downtrodden, and liberate those held in spiritual bondage. They seek the lost and support the saved (3:13; Galatians 6:1-2); no greater cause can be conceived. But without commitment to God's team, neither you nor the church can reach its potential. Sooner or later, your vision will dim, and your passion will grow cold.

That is why the second strategy in your spiritual growth plan should be to identify with a sound congregation. The church provides you with connection, protection and direction. However, you must participate, not just spectate. Ask yourself, what is my contribution to the team? Let me share three essentials for responsible membership in the body of Christ.

Commit to Your Elders

Commitment to the local church requires placing yourself under the direction of its leaders. The men responsible for the overall welfare of a local church are its shepherds, a term synonymous with pastors, bishops, elders or presbyters. They rule over the church in the sense of directing its affairs with the support of a dedicated team of deacons. When the deacons do their job well, the shepherds can devote more time to prayer, study and nurturing people. The bottom line is they watch out for people's souls. Hebrews 13:17 states: "Obey those who rule over you, and be submissive, for they watch out for your souls, as those who must give account. Let them do so with joy and not with grief, for that would be unprofitable for you."

It is not sinful to disagree with your elders or to express a different opinion. The key is to be appropriately assertive and respectful at the same time. Have your say, but do not demand your way. Both you and the church will be blessed when you cooperate with your elders in matters of judgment. Once a decision is made, give the elders your full support. Always put unity above strategy and love before logistics.

When you find it difficult to submit to your elders, keep two things in mind. First, believe that they genuinely care for you. Even when you think they are wrong, they are motivated by love for you and your family. If you misjudge their motives, you will become angry. If you give them the benefit of the doubt (1 Corinthians 13:7), you will feel better even if you disagree. Second, realize that they must consider multiple interests. Their decisions impact many people and often carry unintended consequences. This is why they like to sleep on decisions rather than make snap judgments. When you are disappointed because of a decision they make, stop and consider the interests of others. You may not concur, but you might understand.

The success of any church is tied to the success of its elders, and the success of elders is contingent on the support they are given by members. Paul wrote: "And we urge you, brethren, to recognize those who labor among you, and are over you in the Lord and admonish you, and to esteem them very highly in love for their work's sake. Be at peace among yourselves" (1 Thessalonians 5:12-13). Give your elders plenty of love, respect and appreciation, and you will bless the congregation and yourself. Go to war with your elders, and you will destroy your soul as you divide the church (Matthew 5:9). What could possibly grieve the Holy Spirit more (Ephesians 4:30-32)?

Commit to Church Assemblies

The Bible teaches Christians to gather for worship on the Lord's Day, and Hebrews 10:25 provides a strong warning not to forsake appointed assembly times. Those who neglect worship, study and fellowship drift from Christ and His teaching (2:1). Those who make meeting times a priority grow in "love and good works" (10:24). Faithful attendance is not an arbitrary test of obedience. It is God's means for molding His people. Be sure to take full advantage of the transforming power of church gatherings.

Although most Christians acknowledge the importance of the Sunday morning assembly, some have become indifferent to other gathering times set by the leaders of the church. They are quick to argue that there is no biblical mandate for multiple meeting times. Are other assemblies such as Sunday morning Bible school, Sunday evening worship, and midweek Bible study optional?

Actually, daily gatherings were the practice of the early church. It seems they looked for any reason to spend time together. Their hunger for fellowship was an expression of two things: their need and their joy. Even today, those who really understand what takes place in Christian assemblies yearn for more fellowship rather than less.

The truth is we do what we want and then find reasons to back it up. Neglecting opportunities for growth reveals much about our values. The kinds of questions we ask in making a decision like this are critical. What is best for our families and our brethren? What blessings will we miss by being absent? What is the best use of our time (Ephesians 5:15-16)? By asking the right questions, we will find the right answers. "Do I have to?" is not the right question. "What would God want?" is a better question.

The fact is when you commit to a church, you agree to submit to that church's leadership, and those leaders will most likely request your presence at specified gatherings of the church. They provide these assembly times to help you grow. These elders are your spiritual mentors or shepherds. Therefore, to forsake the assembly is defiant toward your elders (it does not give them joy when you are absent). It is also an offense against God, who gave you spiritual guides only to have you snub His gift (Ephesians 4:8, 11). It hurts your brethren, whom you discourage through your apathy. It sets a poor example for your family. And let me assure you, it hurts you. You will be weaker, not wiser. You will be less like Christ and more like the surrounding culture.

In addition to your congregation's main service times, there are probably a few special activities in which your leaders want everyone to participate. Where I preach, the elders assign every member to one of our C.A.R.E teams. Before Sunday morning worship, the designated team goes to a nearby nursing home to conduct a 30-minute service, which is the highlight of the week for residents. After our congregational worship, the team will host a luncheon to which our visitors are invited. During the post-meal meeting, we sign cards, work on service projects, plan visits, and pray for special needs. The groups also provide food for the sick and bereaved.

There are always some people who do not participate, and perhaps it is not a sin. But they have missed an exceptional growth opportunity and a chance to glorify God by doing good. When I hear the excuses, it makes my heart ache because I know they are depriving themselves of many blessings. Some do not like the menu and are too insecure to bring something different or lead the meal-planning. Others have a non-Christian spouse at home who is waiting on his or her lunch. They lament their inability to win their mates to Christ, not realizing that commitment to such a valuable ministry could be the door God uses to begin life-altering conversations. Seeing your joy and hearing about those you served might help someone see that Christianity is not just about religious services but doing good and growing close in the Lord.

Those who undervalue the benefits of service teams forget that greatness in life consists of little things you do rather than heroic displays of faith on rare occasions. Jesus said whoever gives a cup of cold water in His name will not be forgotten (Mark 9:41). I'm not sure, but I guess the same could be said for handing a nursing home resident a song book and finding the right page for her or signing a card for one who was recently restored or holding someone's hand and praying for an expectant mother on bed rest. And maybe, just maybe, God looks favorably on your commitment to your team despite the fact that you don't like casseroles.

Commit to One Another

The third essential for making a serious commitment to the local church is caring deeply for its members. The church is not brick and mortar: It is people. And what are people but bundles of needs wrapped in flesh and blood? The Roman Emperor Marcus Aurelius remarked, "We are born for cooperation, as are the feet, the hands, the eyelids, and the upper and lower jaws." When you stop and think about it, what could be more obvious? God created people to need people. We were born with needs we could not supply. Therefore, interdependency is part of God's perfect design.

When children are born, they are completely dependent on their parents for food, clothing and shelter. The same neediness can characterize the declining years. Between infancy and old age, many people come to rely on others because of extraordinary circumstances. Deaths, accidents, illnesses and various forms of social upheaval create conditions of neediness.

Yet even the most healthy and productive years are built on mutual dependence. The farmer, tailor, carpenter, merchant, doctor, banker and soldier all count on one another to supply what they cannot provide for themselves. The bonds between citizens in a market economy can be impersonal and driven by self-interest, but Christian fellowship is motivated by compassion and concern for one another's well-being (Acts 2:44-47; 4:32-37). Paul wrote, "Therefore, as we have opportunity, let us do good to all, especially to those who are of the household of faith" (Galatians 6:10).

Followers of Christ cannot remain aloof and detached. In addition to supplying material needs, Christians are alert and responsive to one another's emotional needs. They comfort those who are bereaved and cheer those who are blue (1 Thessalonians 4:18; 5:11). Families know and care for their members, and this natural tendency is intensified in the church by the Spirit of God (Philippians 2:1-2). Those who were strangers are now brothers and sisters in Christ. They "rejoice with those who rejoice, and weep with those who weep" (Romans 12:15).

Christians also tend one another's spiritual needs. They care enough to correct and admonish when needed (Galatians 6:1). By bearing one another's burdens, they "fulfill the law of Christ" (v. 2). They have vital conversations, not just trivial ones. They get real and go deep by speaking truth into one another's lives (Hebrews 3:13).

Team Power in the 21st Century

God worked in teams by using the 12 tribes of Israel to conquer the land of Canaan. Jesus worked in teams by choosing 12 apostles and sending them out two by two. Now the Holy Spirit works in teams by directing churches through the inspired Word. If teams were good enough for the Father, Son and Holy Spirit, perhaps they are good enough to help us achieve our aim of spiritual growth and abundant living.

The real question is not whether teams work but whether you will take your place on God's team to enjoy the benefits He intended. Simply stated, teamwork is less "me" and more "we." It worked for Nehemiah when God's people rebuilt Jerusalem's walls, and it worked for Antioch when missionaries were needed to carry the gospel to distant lands.

When you are added to Jesus' church, you have people on your side who love you, care for your needs, and support your growth. You have this not only for yourself, but also for the family you must guide through this dangerous world. If you could use the power of "we," then deepen your commitment to the local church, and take advantage of the blessings it affords. Doing so will accelerate your growth and multiply your joy. Responsible participation in a sound church is the next faithful step in God's game plan for abundant living.

Questions

1. What makes the parts of Christ's body work together in harmony (1 Corinthians 12:31–13:13)?

2. When does trouble arise in churches?

3. In healthy congregations, what do members value (Philippians 2:3)?

4. In growing congregations, what do members consider (Philippians 2:4)?

5. Outside of the opera, what is a prima donna?

6. What did Margaret Mead say is the only thing that has ever changed the world?

7. Name three things the church provides its members.

8. What are three essentials of responsible church membership?

9. When you find it difficult to submit to your elders, what should you remember?

10. Name three kinds of needs Christians should seek to meet.

For Discussion

1. How can Christians support their elders?

2. What would you do to increase attendance at worship services?

3. How can congregations create a deeper sense of family in the church?

Play of the Day

Write your elders a letter expressing your love, respect and appreciation for what they do on behalf of you and your family.

Growth Strategy #3
Bible Study

"You can't get from A to Z by passing up B."
– Nick Saban – Coach, Alabama Crimson Tide

In all levels of football – high school, college or professional – most drives begin on or around the 20-yard line. With commitment to Christ and His church, you have reached this pivotal point. Now it is time to grind out the yards on your way to God's goal for your life: spiritual maturity.

Commitment to Christ provides the foundation for growth. Commitment to the body of Christ provides support for growth. Now it is time to introduce a third strategy for spiritual development: Commitment to the Word of Christ provides you with direction for growth. Personal Bible study is where all forward progress begins. It is the B on your way from A to Z. Without this, you will never get out of your end of the field and sustain forward movement. Instead, you will suffer a continuous series of setbacks.

Broken Plays and Wasted Days

Broken plays are sometimes the result of outstanding defensive pressure, but more often, the problem is failing to follow the play as designed. Either someone suffered a mental lapse, or even worse, somebody failed to do his homework. The usual outcome is for the ball handler to be tackled for a loss.

In life, as in football, success is contingent upon knowing your game plan. For Christians, that plan is provided in the New Testament. Understanding Christ's teaching is absolutely fundamental to gaining spiritual ground, yet many Christians never develop the discipline of daily Bible study. In the meantime, they wonder why their lives are not working very well. They cannot figure out why they feel spiritually stagnant. The answer is not complicated: Spend more time in God's Word.

Somehow, though, this obvious answer gets overlooked. It seems too simple. Consequently, people search for more complex solutions to their problems. In the meantime, the clock is ticking, and time is running out. The sooner you return to the pathway of spiritual growth, the more you will enjoy life, and the more useful you will be in God's service. So do not waste another minute.

How to Commit to Bible Study

There are three critical components to developing the holy habit of daily Bible study. You need a why, a when and a where.

Why Should I Study?

Knowing you should study the Bible is not enough to build this discipline into your daily routine. Just ask yourself, how many things do I know I ought to do but neglect anyway? So before discussing ways to support this goal, it is vital to appreciate why this commitment matters in the first place. I want to provide you with positive and practical reasons for giving an all-out effort to establish this new practice.

There are at least four good reasons why you should want to study your Bible every day.

(1) Study is commanded by God (Colossians 3:16).
(2) The Bible is reliable and completely true (John 17:17).
(3) Scripture has saving power (2 Timothy 3:15).

These are strong motivations for digging deep into God's Word, but the incentive I want to stress is a little different:

(4) Because it works (2 Timothy 3:16-17).

You derive immediate and practical benefits by embracing Christ's teachings in the Bible. Wisdom is readily available for anyone who hungers for a better life. If you are tired of the disappointing, self-defeating experiences that have come your way in the past, it is time to break the cycle of despair and get on a new path that leads where you want to go.

Daily Bible study is the sure foundation of a satisfying life. Jesus said, "Therefore whoever hears these sayings of Mine, and does them, I will liken him to a wise man who built his house on the rock" (Matthew 7:24). Establishing a devotional time will lift your mind to a higher plane and set you on a spiritual platform for success. Daily study will not rid your life of all problems, but it will provide you with the tools and perspective you need to handle whatever comes your way.

And be certain of this: You will never grow until you make a commitment to develop this discipline. A football player cannot execute the coach's strategy if he never studies his playbook. Similarly, a person cannot live the Christian life apart from an intimate knowledge of Jesus' teachings. To live abundantly and effectively, Bible study is indispensable.

All the good stuff you desire and that God wants you to enjoy lie on the other side of this habit. What do you long for in life?

- Better character?
- Greater influence?
- More usefulness?
- Increased peace?

God promises all of these things and more. Even your material needs will be supplied when you seek first His kingdom and righteousness (Matthew 6:33). But how can you claim to be a serious seeker without spending 5 minutes a day investigating His will?

When Should I Study?

If you struggle to establish the habit of daily Bible study, you have probably never made it a true priority in your life. Your desire to study Scripture is competing against a host of equally powerful desires that push it to the sidelines as soon as your attention is diverted.

For example, during your days in high school, your thirst for spiritual knowledge struggled against homework, extra-curricular activities, dating and a deep yearning to be popular with your friends. In college, your craving for spiritual wisdom vied against pledging a social club, late-night cram sessions, and working two jobs (when you were not attending class). After rigorous preparation for a career, you had to pay your dues to be recognized in your field. Then dating gave way to the demands of family life and caring for the needs of a spouse and children. At first you struggled to get by financially, but as things improved, affluence brought its own set of problems. The new house required more furniture, upkeep and expense; it took nearly a year to unpack the last box and hang the final picture.

Suffice it to say you will never find it convenient to establish the habit of daily Bible reading. There will always be pressure to spend your time in other ways. The only way to succeed is to make your devotional time a higher priority than everything it competes against (Ephesians 5:16). If something has to go, it will not be your time in God's Word. That is simply nonnegotiable.

You may be busy, but with a little effort, you can find time to read one chapter a day. Could you trade 10 minutes of sleep to spend time with God? Is there a part of your morning routine you could sacrifice for Christ? If you bring work home with you, would it ruin your career if you refused to start that project for your manager until you spent a few minutes with your Maker? Do not let mundane things keep you from enjoying the best things in life. Make room for what really matters.

When choosing a time for your devotional, sooner is better than later. If you were a coach, would you like players to study their playbooks before or after the game? Those who begin their day in God's Word have a strategic advantage over those who do not. By studying early, their minds are focused on God from the very start. In addition, they find more opportunities to read throughout the day. It is like building a savings nest egg: Once you do a little, it attracts more.

Finding a routine that fits your lifestyle may take several attempts. Experiment freely, find what works, and pass it on. Maybe your secret is feeding your soul before feeding your body. Perhaps it is opening God's Word before opening your mail. There are many techniques for building this habit, but the important thing is to choose one and give it a chance.

Where Should I Study?

In this technological age, numerous aids can assist you in developing your devotional life. Those who are not digital disciples can rely on simpler prompts to create this new habit. If you own more than one Bible, leave one in your car, where it will be accessible in case you are stuck somewhere with time on your hands. Or buy a small New Testament you can carry with you in your briefcase or shoulder bag.

At home, you may want to leave a Bible on your kitchen table or the counter where you eat breakfast. Use a bookmark to keep your place, or better yet, leave it open to the next reading. What a wonderful message to family members of your love for God and His Word. The key is to leave it where you can see it with ease.

When you make your bed in the morning, place your Bible on the bed, where it will trigger your memory before going to sleep. If you cannot get in bed without handling the book, you are guaranteed to not forget. Or perhaps you can put it by the remote in your den. You know you will touch the remote sometime during the day, and your Bible will be right there. Promise yourself you will read one chapter before turning on the set.

You may want to select a special place that puts you in an optimal frame of mind for communing with God. That could be on your patio, where you feel the wind on your face and sense God's presence. Jesus often retreated to the Garden of Gethsemane. Perhaps there is a park bench near a fountain, stream or pond close to your workplace. Maybe your favorite spot is inside your house: a comfy recliner with a lamp over your shoulder or a quiet office where you can shut the door to interruptions. Mine is a red swivel chair in our den that faces away from the television. Having a predetermined time and place to study increases the odds you will follow through on your goal.

On days you cannot make it to that special place, be flexible, and have a recovery plan. You know there will be days when the unexpected upsets your routine. Be prepared for this, and do not leave your backup reading plan to chance. With a little forethought, you will seldom miss a day in God's Word or suffer the spiraling effects of a life out of touch with the Spirit. When something is this important, your heart will find a way to fulfill its longing. The way will appear when the goal is dear.

If you read one chapter a day Monday through Friday, you can finish the New Testament in a year. When you fall behind, weekends are a great time to catch up on your reading plan. Invite your spouse to join you for an inexpensive date at a local coffee house. Reading your Bible is a duty, but it does not have to be drudgery. Make it fun, and you'll get it done.

Conclusion

If God's game plan for your growth is so straightforward, so sure to succeed, and so simple to implement, how do you account for so few people following through and establishing this daily practice? The answer can be found in the thorny ground of the parable of the sower (Matthew 13:7, 22). When you crowd your schedule with activities and commitments that do not serve your highest interests, something has to give.

Imagine a stream flowing through a lush forest. Although one small rock or stick won't do much to alter its course, a collection of rocks and debris can stop the flow completely. When life becomes too busy, the clutter can block God's blessings. To restore the flow, it is necessary to remove what is clogging the spiritual tributaries of your heart. Reclaim your spiritual health by simplifying your life and prioritizing your schedule. Recouping 5 sacred minutes can change your entire life.

Committed football players guard against distractions that interfere with their preparation and performance. Likewise, Christians must discipline their lives and prioritize their schedules to be their best. Choosing to huddle with God's Word at the start of each day can vastly improve your play on the field of life. Daily Bible study is not the whole answer, but it is the beginning from which every good thing will follow. So understand this: No matter what else you do, you cannot grow to maturity until the Word of Christ dwells in you richly (Colossians 3:16). Sooner or later, you must come to terms with this requirement to live a victorious life. Why not begin now?

Questions

1. What provides a Christian with a foundation for growth?

2. What provides a Christian with support for growth?

3. What provides a Christian with direction for growth?

4. If daily Bible study will not rid your life of all problems, what will it do?

5. In life as in football, success is contingent upon knowing what?

6. What three things do you need to build the practice of daily Bible study?

7. Name four reasons to study your Bible every day.

8. What could an open Bible on the breakfast table communicate?

9. Which parable explains why building good habits is difficult?

10. Name two things Christians can do to become spiritually healthy.

For Discussion

1. How can Bible study help you get more of what you want in life?

2. If you do not read the Bible on a daily basis, what are some activities in your routine you could give up in order to do so?

3. Decide on a time and place where you could study the Bible daily, if you have not already done so.

4. Describe a recovery plan should you miss your regular study time.

Play of the Day

Sometime today, place an open Bible within arm's reach of your favorite breakfast spot. Make sure it is open to the next day's reading. Tell family members not to disturb it even if company is coming over.

Growth Strategy #4
Prayer

**"The difference between ordinary and
extraordinary is that little extra."**
– Jimmy Johnson, Coach, Dallas Cowboys

Prayer is that little "extra" that makes the difference between
an ordinary and extraordinary life. It is the difference between what you can do on your own and what you are capable of with God's help. It is the difference between a day when
you are focused and fervent and a day when you are frantic and
fatigued. One of the great mysteries of life is why so few people
avail themselves of the power of prayer.

The amount of information the Bible contains on the subject
of prayer is amazing. The sheer volume reveals its importance.
Moreover, you can find an incredible number of books written
on the topic. Still, the source of the most original, authoritative
and helpful instruction on prayer remains the Bible. In God's
Word you will find a variety of incentives to practice this daily
discipline. There are

- Commands to engage in prayer (1 Thessalonians 5:17).
- Stories to encourage prayer (Luke 18:1-8).
- Examples of effective prayers (James 5:17-18).
- Promises of the benefit of prayer (Proverbs 15:29).

Principles of Prayer

To get started praying, there are two important things to keep in mind: First, prayer should be offered to the Father, and second, prayer should be offered through the Son.

To the Father

Prayer, in its most basic form, is simply talking to God, but it is easy to lose sight of this fact. The awesomeness of the experience can overwhelm you and complicate what should be a stirring, although straightforward, act. Directing prayer to God means you recognize His unsurpassed interest in your welfare and His unlimited power to assist you. Most of all, it means your chief concern is to please Him.

When praying in Gethsemane, Jesus closed with these words: "Nevertheless, not as I will, but as You will" (Matthew 26:39). In the model prayer, He stated: "Your kingdom come. Your will be done on earth as it is in heaven" (6:10). The idea is that the purpose of prayer should serve the purpose of life: to please and glorify God. Using these expressions is a humble admission that God knows what is best and is committed to what is best for you. To ask for God's will to be done is a sign of maturity, but the real challenge is to mean it.

Spiritual growth and success are the result of putting God's perfect will before your own will. When you trust God so much that you ask Him to overrule your requests, you receive protection from the damaging effects of your sinful nature. By sincerely asking God to override your misguided appeals, the door is opened to new and better possibilities. Just admitting that your way may not be best is a gigantic step forward in spiritual development. Spiritual maturity comes from admitting that

- His heart is pure, and mine is corrupt.
- His interests are broad, and mine are narrow.
- His knowledge is infinite, and mine is limited.
- His perspective is eternal, and mine is temporal.

Through the Son

The second thing to remember is that prayer should be offered through God's Son. This matters because it corresponds to the reality of the situation. Man is helpless to save himself or correct his condition on his own. Jesus is man's Savior and Advocate. Apart from Him, there is no living hope or lasting help. Yet more is involved in invoking Jesus' name than recognizing His role as Redeemer and Intercessor.

To offer prayer in Jesus' name is to do so on His behalf and in harmony with His will. It is not an incantation that guarantees idle wishes will be granted. Rather, it is reminiscent of Paul's appeal to the Colossians: "And whatever you do in word or deed, do all in the name of the Lord Jesus, giving thanks to God the Father through Him" (Colossians 3:17). Paul was not suggesting people go through their day announcing that each completed task on their to-do lists was accomplished in Christ's name. Instead, he was asking the Colossians to conform their words and deeds to Jesus' will. Their lives should be consistent with and representative of Christ.

Unfortunately, many prayers are unreasonable requests for God to rearrange the universe for the petitioner's comfort or convenience. They express flesh-based, ego-driven desires. When a person comes before the Father in Jesus' name asking for what is truly right, he approaches God's throne with absolute certainty of receiving help in time of need. He does not come alone, and He does not come timidly. He approaches the mercy seat with full assurance of Christ's presence and promises (Hebrews 10:22).

To live life under the authority of Christ is more than affirming His rank above every power and principality. It is believing that His way is the right way. The authority Jesus enjoys is not limited to the positional power found in human organizations (governments and corporations). It is the inherent power of His ideals to bless people's lives. Therefore, to pray in Jesus' name is to seek His help in bringing life into conformity with His perfect will. It is the same as asking for God's will to be done. It is seeking first God's kingdom and His righteousness (Matthew 6:33).

Topics of Prayer

The acronym ACTS is often used to teach new Christians how to pray. The letters represent four of the most common themes of prayer: adoration, confession, thanksgiving and supplication. Prayer cannot be reduced to a simple list, but it is helpful to understand why these concerns are central to Christian living and communion with God.

Adoration: Remember Who Is Listening

Opening prayer with adoration prepares your mind for what follows. The Lord's model prayer begins, "Our Father in heaven, hallowed be Your name" (Matthew 6:9). Recalling that God is heavenly and holy puts everything into perspective. Heavenliness speaks of His capacity, and holiness speaks of His character. By verbalizing these ideas over and over, you imprint them on your soul. When children pray "God is great, God is good," it instills confidence in His power and love. You are ready to face anything the day may bring when you are certain of these truths.

Calling God "Father" is a reminder of His love. It speaks of His wisdom and of His nearness and concern. The Lord welcomes you into His presence, and lingering is encouraged. No limitation is placed on the number of visits or their duration. God is not remote and uncaring. He is in your corner pulling for you. Like a caring parent, He wants to help you construct an honorable, useful and fulfilling life. However, receiving God's help depends on believing it is available and asking for it.

Confession: Remember Who Is Talking

When coming before God in prayer, the instinctive response of an adoring heart is to confess sin. Dwelling on God's magnificence makes you increasingly aware of your own weakness and sinfulness. When Isaiah glimpsed God's glory, his immediate response was to blurt out words of contrition: "Woe is me, for I am undone! Because I am a man of unclean lips, and I dwell in the midst of a people of unclean lips; for my eyes have seen the King, the LORD of hosts" (Isaiah 6:5).

Peter had a similar experience while fishing with Jesus one day. The outing was astonishingly successful. As Peter hauled in the catch, he had a flash of insight that made him shudder in his soul. He realized no natural explanation could account for the incredible results that day. Instantly, he knew He was in the presence of God's Son, and a deep sense of unworthiness swept over him. Peter fell down at Jesus' knees and cried, "Depart from me, for I am a sinful man" (Luke 5:8).

The natural response after heartfelt praise for God is confession of sin. Jesus illustrated this point in a story about a tax collector who came to the temple to worship the Lord. I envision the scene this way. After getting there, he found himself practically speechless. His shaking legs would not carry him the last few steps to join the other petitioners. He could not hold his head erect, and his eyelids refused to open as he labored to express the feelings of his burdened heart. Nearing emotional exhaustion, he beat his breast in a desperate attempt to speak. Even then, he could manage only a few words: "God, be merciful to me a sinner!" (Luke 18:13-14). Although he may have felt embarrassed by his lack of eloquence and composure, God was pleased. The man went home justified. God loves humble hearts and penitent prayers because He knows the foundation of spiritual growth is recognizing your need for help and asking for it.

Thanksgiving: Remember How Blessed You Are

Prayer and appreciation are partners in spiritual growth (Philippians 4:6). Consequently, prayer should be a continual pleasure, not just a last resort. Every blessing you enjoy should bring to mind its benefactor. When this is true, giving thanks becomes as natural as breathing. Prayer produces constant joy by drawing you closer to the source of all joy.

One of the benefits of thankfulness is that it produces a spirit of hopefulness. When you reflect on what God has done for you in the past, you grow more sure of the future. The residue of gratitude is confidence. Joy and optimism are but lingering traces of God's past blessings.

Supplication: Remember How Needy You Are

Your Maker is more concerned about your future than anyone, including your mate and your mama. Moreover, He is prepared to supply whatever you need to grow and mature. Unfortunately, many Christians withhold legitimate prayer requests believing they are too trivial to bring before God. Peter urged you to bring all your cares (1 Peter 5:7). If it is pressing on your heart, God wants to hear about it. How many children needlessly struggle with problems that easily could be resolved if they would open up to a loving parent? Likewise, God wants you to open up to Him, and you can rest assured no person has ever exhausted the resources of the heavenly Father.

We do not come enough, and we do not ask enough. Moreover, the margins of what we are missing are mind-boggling. Paul scolded the Ephesians for their puny prayers by reminding them God was able to do much more than they were asking or could even imagine (Ephesians 3:20). Most people use only a tiny portion of their prayer power. The sad fact is God is infinite, accessible and ignored.

The only prayer request prohibited by God is a selfish one. James explained, "You ask and do not receive, because you ask amiss, that you may spend it on your pleasures" (James 4:3). In other words, if what you ask for will do you harm rather than good, God says, "No way." What else would you expect from a loving father? If a child asks for a rattlesnake to play with or a gallon of ice cream for a bedtime snack, what is a parent to do? The answer is easy for a wise father and difficult for a weak one.

God is more concerned about your well-being than whether you like Him at any given moment. He cannot be emotionally blackmailed. He is too strong and too good for that. But make no mistake, when a prayer request is holy and healthy, God is more than happy to comply. When your will aligns with His will, the floodgates of heaven open, and cups start running over.

The Spirit of Prayer

Instruction in the mechanics of prayer has its place, but care must be taken to capture the spirit of prayer, not just its forms. The important thing in prayer is not length, loudness or literary quality. The principal thing is not a precise formula of words, a checklist of subjects, or a position of the body. It is mindfulness of the Father and the Son in all that you say and do. It is harmonizing your thoughts with Their thoughts and your will with Their will. When this is the case, you cannot remain upset when circumstances do not conform to your liking.

Rather than grumbling, the thoughtful petitioner returns to the Father in gratitude for His perfect will. It takes real maturity to acknowledge that God's timing and solutions are superior to your own. He will do what is best when it is best; therefore, modifications to your prayer requests should be welcomed as improvements, not viewed as impositions. When you learn to appreciate this truth, you are well on your way to living a more abundant life.

Questions

1. What is one of the greatest mysteries of all time?

2. Name four ways the Bible encourages people to pray.

3. Name two important things to remember about offering prayer.

4. What is prayer in its most basic form?

5. Name three things implied by directing prayer to God.

6. How did Jesus close His prayer in Gethsemane (Matthew 26:39)?

7. Asking for God's will to be done is a sign of what?

8. Failing to pray is a clear admission of what?

9. What do the letters in the acronym "ACTS" stand for?

10. Modifications to prayer requests should be welcomed as what?

For Discussion

1. How do you think your life would change if you prayed more?

2. What are some ways you can improve your prayer life?

3. How do you think you would feel if you spent more time praying?

Play of the Day

Commit to praying the ACTS prayer every day for a week. To get started, have four men lead the class in prayer, each focusing on a different component of the acronym (adoration, confession, thanksgiving or supplication).

Discipline

**"Without self-discipline,
success is impossible, period."**
– Lou Holtz, Coach, Notre Dame

To become a stellar athlete or devoted Christian, no quality is more important than self-control. It appears last among the fruit of the Spirit because self-regulation is the quality that guarantees all that precede it (Galatians 5:22-23). Ungodliness and unhappiness result from losing control in some part of your life (vv. 19-21). Without self-control there can be little love, joy or peace. Therefore, the decisive factor in leading a fruitful life is the ability to exercise control over your thoughts, words and deeds. Discipline is the link between your dreams and your destiny.

People who can will themselves to act or refrain from acting enjoy greater success than those who live at the mercy of their urges and emotions. For a football player, self-discipline is necessary for physical conditioning, learning offensive plays and defensive formations, avoiding penalties that hurt the team, and maintaining academic eligibility. For people of faith, self-discipline is necessary for resisting temptation and persevering through trials. It enables you to hold your tongue and govern your temper. It also promotes spiritual growth and selfless service. In other words, self-discipline empowers you to live proactively and positively rather than reactively and negatively. Impulse control is the linchpin to living well.

Many of the Bible's saddest events resulted from a lack of self-control. Adam and Eve ate forbidden fruit (Genesis 3:6). Cain killed Abel (4:8). Noah got drunk (9:20-21). David committed adultery (2 Samuel 11:2-5). The pattern is clear: Lack of discipline is the basis of sin and most of the world's unhappiness.

In contrast, Jesus' teaching was a call for self-mastery. The Sermon on the Mount was a plea for disciplined, ethical living (Matthew 5–7). The apostles urged Christians to reject worldliness and follow Jesus' holy restraint and devotion to doing good. Paul preached on self-control to political leaders (Acts 24:25) and church leaders alike (Titus 1:8). Clearly, self-regulation is essential for successful living, and it is possible through God's grace.

> For the grace of God that brings salvation has appeared to all men, teaching us that, denying ungodliness and worldly lusts, we should live soberly, righteously and godly in the present age, looking for the blessed hope and glorious appearing of our great God and Savior Jesus Christ, who gave Himself for us, that He might redeem us from every lawless deed and purify for Himself His own special people, zealous for good works. (Titus 2:11-14)

Control Is Possible

Proverbs warns, "Whoever has no rule over his own spirit is like a city broken down, without walls" (25:28). Healthy boundaries provide a wall of defense against destructive forces that threaten your highest interests and noblest pursuits. Discipline is the security system of the soul. Without it, your hopes and dreams are placed at risk.

You interact with the surrounding world through your choices. Those choices create your experience of life. Parents and peers influence your decisions, but you decide your future (Proverbs 9:12). Your mind is active rather than passive, and your will is free rather than enslaved. You do not act out every impulse. You choose how far you will go to get what you want. Understanding that control is possible. Let's look at some practical ways to take back the reins of your life.

Keys to Control

Self-control does not happen by chance. You must desire it and develop it. To become a more disciplined person and enjoy a more abundant life, put these proven strategies to work.

Purpose

In the parable of the sower, Jesus used rocky ground to illustrate the danger of low commitment (Luke 8:6, 13). When the heat turns up, only those with deep roots (dedication) can survive. Casual interest in Jesus' teaching will not do. You must submit to the Lord's authority with a glad heart (John 8:31). Purpose to please Him, and you will find it easier to live a disciplined life.

Prioritize

A second key to self-control is knowing what you want and why you want it (Philippians 1:20). When the reasons for pursuing a goal are clear and compelling, you drastically increase your chances of success. The greater your incentive, the greater your effort and endurance. Motivation stirs passion, and passion fuels progress.

Plan

When you are vague about your plans, it is difficult to turn longings into action. When you are clear about your path, forward progress becomes predictable (Proverbs 21:5). Therefore, the more you prepare in advance, the less dependent you are on a limited supply of willpower to accomplish your goals. Serious people rely more on preparation than iron will. Advanced planning does not solve every problem, but it makes things a lot easier.

Pray

The more focused you are, the greater your chances of success. When you set a goal, write it down, post it where you will see it, and then pray about it every day. Prayer can turn a passing interest into a top priority. Goals cannot thrive in the shadows of competing interests. The solution is to shine the spotlight of prayer on your most cherished dream, and give it center stage. Supplication and self-regulation go hand in hand.

Practice

If you want more of something in your life (like self-control), you have to practice it. The more you practice, the more you accelerate your growth. For example, a field goal kicker must practice field goals. Desire gets him started, but only practice can make him better. In time, good routines turn into good abilities. Discipline is a lifeskill developed through deliberate practice.

Persevere

Fortitude is the capstone of a disciplined life. To develop more staying power, be more selective about your commitments. Over-committing weakens your will and compromises what is truly important. By counting the cost upfront, you reduce recurring internal debates. When discouraging voices pop into your head, the less you debate and delay, the better your chances of success. When you think you have reached the end of your rope, it is just your fears talking. There are options untried and power untapped. When things gets tough, dig deep inside to keep going. Remember, the infinite Spirit is your helper, and the resources of the Almighty are at your disposal.

Areas in Need of Control

Spiritual Living

Commitments to church assemblies and private devotions supply you with strength for growth and achievement. Spiritual disciplines accomplish this by heightening the Spirit's influence in your life. Paul wrote:

> And do not be drunk with wine, in which is dissipation; but be filled with the Spirit, speaking to one another in psalms and hymns and spiritual songs, singing and making melody in your heart to the Lord, giving thanks always for all things to God the Father in the name of our Lord Jesus Christ, submitting to one another in the fear of God. (Ephesians 5:18-21)

Being under the influence of alcohol gives you less control. Being under the influence of the Spirit gives you more control. Joy and unity come from time in the Bible, not the bottle. They come from being thankful, considerate and reverent as the Spirit teaches in God's Word.

Healthy Living

Plenty of rest, moderate exercise and good nutrition provide the energy you need to engage life at full capacity. Deprived of these, your brain and body function at diminished levels. Self-discipline allows you to work in harmony with the way God made you. No doubt, some health issues are beyond your control, but these three are definitely your responsibility.

(1) Rest: One of the best things you can do to develop more self-control is to go to bed and get up at set times. A full night's sleep improves your focus and endurance. Sleep deprivation leaves you feeling foggy and tired. It is hard to be dedicated or disciplined when you can barely hold your head up.

(2) Exercise: Strength, stamina and flexibility are signs of vitality. When you maximize your physical health, you feel better and think clearer. Start slow, increase gradually, and skip the pain and discouragement of rapid starts and stops.

(3) Nutrition: Eating wisely will not only extend your life but will improve your quality of life. It is not a sin to savor good food, but it is wrong to damage the body God entrusted to your care. Do not worship at the altar of your taste buds. Live to please your Savior, not your stomach (Philippians 3:19).

Holy Living

The Bible ultimately teaches you should bring your entire life into submission to Christ. But these three areas – your mouth, money and moods – are a good place to start and are essential for well-being.

(1) Your Mouth: The greatest opportunity for developing self-control rests with your speech because it is easy to monitor, and the practice opportunities are plentiful. Inopportune words hurt people's feelings and damage relationships. When you catch yourself judging, gossiping, exaggerating, misleading or complaining, ask yourself, what need am I trying to satisfy by engaging in this destructive behavior? Note the circumstances to see if you can spot triggers or trends (person, time, place or situation). Think of what you will say or do differently next time. Try rehearsing your next encounter. According to Paul, the test for all speech is whether it edifies and imparts grace (Ephesians 4:29). The more you encourage people and build them up, the sooner you take back control of your life.

(2) **Your Money:** Exercising self-control in handling money is one of the most spiritual things you will ever do. Your checkbook register is a window into your soul. It tells the story of your true values and priorities. Paul taught that covetousness is a form of idolatry (Colossians 3:5). That is to say, it can become the controlling force in your life (Ephesians 4:28). It can turn you into a criminal, workaholic, spendthrift or miser. Paul warned, "Those who desire to be rich fall into temptation and a snare, and into many foolish and harmful lusts which drown men in destruction and perdition" (1 Timothy 6:9).

No matter how much money you have, there is wisdom in living on a budget. It keeps you mindful of the difference between your needs and wants. It helps you save for emergencies without diminishing your charitable giving. It is a reminder that you are a steward of your wealth for which you must give an account. Disciplined giving, saving and spending ensure that money remains your servant and not your master (v. 18).

(3) **Your Moods**: On the worst day of Jesus' life, He kept His control. He did not lash out even when wrongfully arrested, falsely convicted and mercilessly crucified. Do your emotions control you, or do you control your emotions? Difficult times are not an excuse for irritability and nastiness. Paul said, "Do not let the sun go down on your wrath" (Ephesians 4:26). This command proves you can limit the intensity and duration of angry feelings. It is simply a choice. Too often, however, we prefer to nurse grudges rather than heal them. Paul urged Christians not to give in to this temptation:

And do not grieve the Holy Spirit of God, by whom you were sealed for the day of redemption. Let all bitterness, wrath, anger, clamor, and evil speaking be put away from you, with all malice. And be kind to one another, tenderhearted, forgiving one another, even as God in Christ forgave you. (Ephesians 4:30-32)

By switching your thoughts from your grievance to God's grace, your mood can quickly improve. Better thoughts are the key to a better temperament (2 Corinthians 10:5).

Limits of Control

A great deal of frustration occurs when you make yourself responsible for people or events that are beyond your control. Attempting the impossible can only lead to disappointment. For instance, you have little control over the climate or economy. Worrying about Wall Street and complaining about the weather do nothing to change your circumstances. It also annoys the people around you. How much better to carry an umbrella and diversify your savings. Don't fuss – adjust!

Attempting to control people is especially exasperating. You can influence others, but you cannot control them. Making demands of your mate is less effective than making requests. Bossing your kids is less effective than coaching. High expectations and accountability are beneficial, but being domineering and imperious are not. The key to successful relationships is learning to control yourself rather than others. Nagging, threatening and yelling mercly prove that you lack composure. Reasoning, persuasion and negotiation demonstrate respect and create goodwill. The fruit of the Spirit is control of *self*, not control of others.

Hindrances to Self-Control

What are you allowing to control you that is not helping? What distracts your mind, depletes your energy, and discourages your heart? When you find the answer, make a correction. One thing is for certain: Your life cannot change until you do.

Digital Distractions

Technology has changed the world of communication, organization, transportation, commerce and entertainment (not always for the better). It can consume time as well as save it, and it can erode character as well as improve it. It all depends on how you use it.

Indiscriminate TV-viewing can debase and depress you. Injudicious use of the Internet can corrupt you and lead to addictive behavior. Media that is delivered cheaply, instantly and privately to your favorite device can be a danger or a blessing. Even wholesome content can dominate your life and disconnect you from your family and reality. An occasional technology fast can help you keep your perspective, and self-monitoring is vital to protect your values and relationships. Ask yourself, do I have healthy boundaries in my use of technology?

Unhealthy Relationships

Face it, some people drag you down (1 Corinthians 15:33). When you are around them, you lose control. In their presence, you are more likely to give in and go along rather than grow. Limit your exposure to companions who diminish or discourage you. Minister to everyone you can, but look for faith and character when choosing intimate allies. You will know them because they will bring out your best. Healthy relationships provide you with encouragement and accountability to live an honorable, useful life.

Overcommitting

If you have a servant spirit, this may be your toughest challenge. You love to help people, but your time and energy are limited. When you overcommit, something always suffers: your family, your health or the quality of your work. The truth is you are little good to anyone when your obligations exceed your capacity. Do not take on more unless you have the time and energy to make a wholehearted commitment. Ask the advice of your spouse or a close friend before obligating yourself. Never make a long-term commitment without sleeping on it and praying about it first.

Impatience

Attempting too much too soon is a major barrier to fulfilled dreams. Take workouts for example: Attempting to go from zero to hero overnight can produce the opposite result of what you want. The problem is not too much zeal. The problem is how you channel it. Impulsiveness is enthusiasm out of control. The challenge is to manage your energy for the long haul. Find your pace, and leave some gas in your tank for the fourth quarter.

Discouragement

When multiple areas of your life spiral out of control, it can be debilitating. You feel overwhelmed, unable to take any action. The solution is to retake control of one small area of your life. The good feelings you derive will arm you with confidence and motivation to do more. Little by little, you will create a snowball effect that will generate irresistible momentum for taking positive action.

Besetting Sins

Is there a secret sin you have not licked? Maybe you have suppressed it but have not overcome it. Does it gnaw at your soul and fill you with guilt and anxiety? Do you spend more time recovering from setbacks than moving forward in life? Until you deal this urge a death blow, it will hold you back from becoming the best person you can be. It is time to get it in the open. Find a trusted elder, minister, friend, therapist or family member to help you. Imagine what life will be like when you resolve this issue in your heart. All that energy can be reclaimed and reinvested in something positive that will magnify God. Quit playing around. Get serious. You have the power.

Your future happiness and success cannot be greater than the degree of control you exercise over your life. As you gain control, your prospects brighten. As you lose control, your future dims. Demonstrations of love are the highest expressions of self-control (John 15:13). With that thought in mind, it is time to begin part two of this book. From self-mastery, we now turn to spiritual ministry.

Questions

1. Why is self-control listed last among the fruit of the Spirit?

2. Name two results of losing control over your life.

3. What do the saddest stories in the Bible have in common?

4. Name three crucial areas for developing good health habits.

5. Name three areas you must learn to control for your well-being.

6. What is a leading cause of anxiety and frustration?

7. What is more effective than making demands of your peers?

8. What is more effective than bossing children?

9. When you feel overwhelmed, what is the solution?

10. What are the highest expressions of self-control?

For Discussion

1. How does lack of discipline complicate your life?

2. How can more discipline improve your life?

3. How can you increase your self-discipline?

Play of the Day

Pick one area where you would like to be more disciplined. What are your reasons for choosing this area? Make sure your choice is within your control; then write a plan for taking control of this part of your life. In writing your plan, refer back to the "Keys to Control" on page 69 and the "Hindrances to Self-Control" on page 73. After formulating your plan, answer this question: What is my next step? Then do it as soon as possible without debate or delay.

Ministry

Growth Strategies 6-10: Giving Back

"It was great to win the Super Bowl, but really and truly what you're going to leave on this earth is the influence on others."
– Joe Gibbs, Coach, Washington Redskins

The time has come to cross midfield and move from self-mastery to spiritual ministry. By taking control of your life, you are ready to put it to good use. Mastery provided you with a sense of peace and order. Now ministry will increase your feelings of usefulness and fulfillment. By helping others, you will please God, grow more Christlike, and make a positive difference in the world.

The second half of this book presents five strategies for growing spiritually by investing your life in others. It all begins with cultivating the virtues that enhance interpersonal relationships (the fruit of the Spirit). From there, we will examine how Christians contribute to the lives of others through serving, giving and sharing their faith. Finally, we will consider the importance of perseverance, the crowning quality of successful people and the final tactic in God's game plan for abundant life.

Growth Strategy #6
Virtue

**"We are all born naked into this world,
but each of us is fully clothed in potential."**
– Emmitt Smith, Running Back, Dallas Cowboys

Crossing midfield gives an offensive team a boost in confidence. The defense is back on its heels. The quarterback feels the momentum shifting his way. The same is true with your progress in Christian living. As you gain more control over your life, you sense a readiness to move into new territory.

The first five growth strategies focused mostly on you. The immediate goal was to establish a foundation for a stable life through self-mastery. God's game plan began with growth in commitment, fellowship, Bible study, prayer and discipline.

The next five growth strategies will move you closer to your overall goal of abundant living. You will move out of your end of the field into the territory of others. But remember: New levels of joy require new levels of dedication. Everything gets more challenging as more people get involved. The remaining strategies require you to grow in virtue, service, giving, evangelism and perseverance.

The Fruit of the Spirit

This chapter will focus on Christian virtues that support healthy relationships. Paul called these qualities the fruit of the Spirit. This sacred list demonstrates that the Holy Spirit is devoted to your improvement as well as your salvation. How does He work?

- His presence challenges you (1 Corinthians 6:18-20).
- His pleading comforts you (Romans 8:26-27).
- His purpose changes you (John 16:8-11).

To walk in the Spirit, you must think like the Spirit. You must choose between pleasing your flesh or your Father. Will sensuality or spirituality define your life?

In the previous chapter, we saw the link between self-discipline and a well-ordered life. Now we will see how it contributes to loving relationships. Paul told the Romans love does no harm to its neighbor (Romans 13:10). Self-control is the restraining power of love. It protects others from injuries that occur in love's absence. Genuine love is expressed in two ways: what you do and what you will not do.

James reasoned that if man can control animals, vehicles and the elements, he also has the capacity for self-direction (James 3:1-6). Still, you must choose whether to avail yourself of the encouragement and assistance God provides for holy living. God sent the Holy Spirit to help you regain control of your thoughts, words, emotions and desires. Because self-control is a fruit of the Spirit, the more God's Spirit is central in your life, the more control you will have. Conversely, the more you try to handle things on your own, the more chaos will ensue.

The key to a great life is setting yourself up for success by creating a superb environment for spiritual growth. Through conversion, you make room for the Holy Spirit in your heart. Through worship and study, you invite Him to mold your mind. Through fellowship with those who walk in the Spirit, you receive encouragement and accountability as you pursue a righteous life (Philippians 2:1-4). Those who fail to study, worship, fellowship and pray cut themselves off from God's power for successful living (Acts 2:40-42). They base their choices on worldly values and then wonder why life is difficult.

Christianity was designed to reactivate your spiritual capacities deadened by sin. A new, better you emerges as the higher part of your nature takes charge. The driving force behind this transformation is more than willpower: It is a new heart, awakened and sanctified by God's Spirit. With His help, you are empowered to reclaim control of your life. However, you will struggle to maintain this control throughout your lifetime. That is why biblical writers portray Christian living as spiritual warfare. Self-control is about mind-control, and the battle for your mind is the fight for your soul's survival. The term "self-control" was not intended to minimize the work of the Spirit. It merely emphasizes that the final responsibility rests with you.

What the Holy Spirit Does

How does the Holy Spirit fortify your will? One thing is certain: He does not miraculously infuse willpower in a way that robs you of freedom. The same Spirit that indwells you (1 Corinthians 3:16) and intercedes for you (Romans 8:26-27) also instructs you through God's Word. To disregard inspired teaching is to cut yourself off from the Holy Spirit and His means of strengthening you. Paul warned, "Therefore he who rejects this does not reject man, but God, who has also given us His Holy Spirit" (1 Thessalonians 4:8). The Spirit knows what is right. Apart from His guidance, humans merely guess.

Study, prayer and obedience are ways to take advantage of the Spirit's work on your behalf. The Holy Spirit will not override your free will. Your spirit must be receptive and cooperative. To walk or live in the Spirit (Galatians 5:16, 25) is to bring your life in line with the teaching of the Bible. The key to a strong will and successful life is to love God's Word and live it. In this way, the Spirit exerts an ever-increasing influence in your life.

Just as with athletes, Christians need discipline to accomplish their personal and spiritual goals (1 Corinthians 9:25). Spiritual growth occurs as you increase your capacity to control your life. It is learning to manage your thoughts, emotions and choices to produce positive outcomes that please God. The absence of self-control results in selfishness, immorality and hostility. The presence of control produces holy living and healthy relationships.

In time, Christians grow more confident in their ability to exercise self-control. Overconfidence is a dangerous thing (1 Corinthians 10:12), but a lack of confidence can be equally harmful (Revelation 21:8). Appropriate levels of confidence are critical for engaging life responsibly. Christians are not weak and powerless (2 Timothy 1:7). Feelings of helplessness are more about unbelief than humility. As your faith grows, so does your confidence (1 Timothy 3:13). It affects what you will attempt, the amount of effort you will put forth, and how long you will endure. Paul declared, "I can do all things through Christ who strengthens me" (Philippians 4:13). The difference between egotism and confidence is dependence on Christ. Every worthwhile achievement is accomplished for His glory and through His aid.

Walking in the Spirit

The phrase "fruit of the Spirit" refers to the results of the Holy Spirit's influence on your life. If the Spirit is to exert an influence on your thinking and behavior, it is essential to maintain a vital connection with Him. Jesus spoke of this ongoing relationship in John 15:4: "Abide in Me, and I in you. As the branch cannot bear fruit of itself, unless it abides in the vine, neither can you, unless you abide in Me." To abide is to stay in close contact with Jesus through heeding His Word (8:31).

To abide is not to lazily lounge in His presence. It cannot be accomplished effortlessly like a plane operating on autopilot. Abiding requires vigorous spiritual activity. It is joyous but strenuous. Jesus' illustration was not meant to convey that spiritual growth occurs without struggle or pain. He was stressing the necessity of a continuing relationship with Him and the results you can expect when you are faithful. You abide in Christ when you live in accordance with His teaching. When you believe Jesus' words and keep them, you remain in Him.

Once a person enters Christ, he must use the means God provided to keep the relationship thriving. Through persistent prayer, your heart merges with His heart. Through continuous study, your mind unites with His mind. Still, you must walk in the Spirit, not merely wait for the Spirit to act on your behalf. Commands call forth intention and effort. Warnings demand vigilance and self-discipline. If holy living is automatic, why did Paul tell Christians not to grieve or quench the Spirit (Ephesians 4:30; 1 Thessalonians

5:19)? Why write to saints about the struggle between the Spirit and flesh (Galatians 5:17)? Why issue any instructions at all?

Walking in the Spirit and abiding in Christ are similar ideas. You cannot do one without the other. The Spirit is the Helper sent by Christ to guide and comfort you as you journey through life. As a true friend, He comes alongside you to assist in appropriate, God-intended ways. He will not interfere with your free will, but He does provide the support you need. He teaches and encourages; you trust and obey. Submission and steadfastness are the duties of saints.

Virtues of the Spirit

Walking in the Spirit is the key to a fruitful life. Whatever your job or role, the virtues of the Spirit make you more effective with people. In fact, you might say Paul was describing virtues of a successful life. Stop and consider how each enhances your relationships with others.

Love

When people sense that you are caring and compassionate, they are more receptive to your influence than if they believe you are heartless and self-serving.

Joy

People are naturally attracted to those who are positive and optimistic, but they quickly tire of pessimists who are perpetually negative and critical.

Peace

Those who bring people together accomplish more than those who sow seeds of discord. Christians prize unity and goodwill over self-promotion and winning at all costs.

Longsuffering

Forbearance and forgiveness provide a healthy environment for positive change. Impatience stunts growth and fosters ill will.

Kindness

People who treat others with thoughtfulness and consideration are appreciated. Those who are disrespectful are resented.

Goodness
People who do good are held in esteem while those who do harm are held in contempt. Christians strive to be useful and add value to those around them.

Gentleness
A soft word and gentle hand enable those in error to receive correction. A harsh word and heavy hand provoke resentment and resistance to change. Nothing is as restorative as gentleness.

Faithfulness
When people believe you are trustworthy and devoted to their well-being, they will go the second mile for you. If they think you are unreliable and self-centered, they will hold back.

Self-Control
An undisciplined person spends his time and energy gratifying his own desires. A disciplined person directs his attention to glorifying God and serving others.

Examples
Consider how these qualities make people more effective in different settings.

Loving spouses are not demanding or demeaning. They enjoy doing things to help their mates reach their potential and fulfill their dreams. **Joyful fathers** are not miserable, frustrated or angry men. Instead, their hopeful outlook makes family members delight in their presence and seek them out for counsel, consolation or good company. **Peace-minded teams** are not plagued by divisiveness. Trust and respect allow members to move beyond their insecurities so they can get down to business. **Longsuffering teachers** are sympathetic with struggling students. They patiently work with pupils to help them improve.

Kind bosses are appropriately assertive but not insensitive or unreasonable. Their courtesy and consideration make them employers of choice. **Good employees** are not wasteful and worthless. They add value to their employers by doing their jobs and going the second mile. **Gentle mothers** are not dictatorial. They hold their children accountable, but their tenderness makes their children more receptive to instruction and correction. **Faithful friends** do not betray those who trust them. They prove themselves dependable and honorable by keeping confidences and maintaining faith in trying times. **Disciplined students** are not lazy and irresponsible. They know how to resist distractions and direct their energy to educational goals.

Change Your Mind, Change Your Life

Whatever your dreams and aspirations, success hinges on your ability to get along with other people. Growth in the Christian virtues improves your ability to relate well. It increases your influence with others so that you can bring God's blessings to their lives. There is no need for fake smiles and flattery. Walking in the Spirit allows you to be authentic and effective at the same time.

Whatever you want to see in your relationships must be visible in your own spirit. Think of your heart as a garden you must tend every day. Your character and, often, your circumstances are the harvest of your labors, and satisfying relationships are the sunflowers of your soul. The more disciplined you are in caring for your garden, the more beautiful it will be.

Success is a result of thinking on a higher level. You cannot improve your life without improving your mind (Romans 12:2). Through prayer and Bible study, the Holy Spirit elevates your thoughts to increase your victories. He does this by making you more honorable and relational. The right spirit is the key to success, and the Holy Spirit is the source of your ability and nobility.

Love's Drawing Power

Jesus said, "And I, if I am lifted up from the earth, will draw all peoples to Myself" (John 12:32). The magnetism of Jesus is an indisputable fact of history. His loving life and lofty ideas have a drawing power without equal in the world. As we lift up Jesus through Christlike living, we draw people closer because they see Him in us. Sin repels and divides people. The fruit of the Spirit attracts and unites people. In addition to preaching Christ, make up your mind to live like Christ to enjoy the quality relationships and abundant life He promised His followers (10:10).

Questions

1. Name the five remaining strategies for spiritual growth.

2. On what does your success usually depend?

3. To walk in the Spirit, what must you do?

4. What is the restraining power of love?

5. How do people cut themselves off from God's power for successful living?

6. Why is the Christian life portrayed as warfare?

7. What three words beginning with "i" describe what the Spirit does?

8. What does it mean to walk in the Spirit?

9. What determines the difference between egotism and confidence?

10. What does the phrase "fruit of the Spirit" mean?

For Discussion

1. Why is lacking confidence as bad as being overconfident?

2. Why is it appropriate to call the virtues of the Spirit "the virtues of a successful life"?

3. How is your heart like a garden?

Play of the Day

Take a few minutes and memorize the nine virtues Paul called the fruit of the Spirit. For the next seven days, recite the list, and then pick out a different quality each day to practice. Pray that people will see Christ in you as you practice these traits. Take note of ways your relationships improve as a result of your efforts.

Growth Strategy #7
Service

"God's definition of success is really one of significance – the significant difference our lives can make in the lives of others"
– Tony Dungy, Coach, Indianapolis Colts

I n football, the turf between an opponent's 40- and 30-yard line is expensive real estate. It is 10 yards worth of heart-pumping thrills. The crowd gets louder, and the players get more physical. Every fan knows that the 30-yard line is field goal territory. Everyone exerts extra effort during this set of downs as the team moves into scoring range.

So it is with your spiritual growth. Moving to the next milestone in God's game plan is where things really get exciting because this step requires intense action, not just quiet contemplation. Serving carries us deep into the territory of people's lives. Here, you will wrestle with your priorities, bump into human pride, and tackle procrastination. Hands get dirty as you deal with real-life needs and desires. This is the land of blood, sweat and tears, where faith undergoes its toughest test to date.

Stretching for the 30-yard line moves you beyond becoming to doing. Your attention shifts dramatically to caring for your fellow man. The purpose of everything to this point was to prepare you for this moment. Why study, pray, worship and fellowship? God's plan is to use these experiences to transform you into His emissary, fully equipped to reach hurting and discouraged people with the gospel. Developing a servant's heart readies you to engage the world at the critical point of its unmet needs.

The Two-Sided Coin

Christianity is not only about cultivating good character, but doing good deeds that manifest that character (Hebrews 10:22). Those who reduce religion to negatives are missing out on the best God has to offer. Holiness is a two-sided coin.

The works of the flesh must be avoided, and failure to do so carries real penalties. When a football player violates a rule of the game, the official throws a yellow flag and marches off negative yardage, but the consequences of sin are deeper and more personal. When a Christian breaks God's law, he loses ground in his efforts to reach spiritual maturity and to become an effective servant of Christ.

However, the Christian faith is more than a spiritual do and don't list. The reason God tells people not to do certain things is because they are the opposite of what He wants for their lives. God's goal is for you to become one big breathing blessing, and sin does not serve that purpose. Sin hurts you and throws you off course at the same time. It not only stops you in your tracks, but also backs you up as you regress spiritually. And just as in football, every inch of lost ground must be made up to get back to the original line of scrimmage. In life, penalties are not punishments but teachers. They tell us where we need to go back and relearn how to respect ourselves and treat others so we can move forward in life.

The Ultimate Example of Service

Holiness is about purity, but it is also about mercy. Those who want to follow Jesus but do not want to serve misunderstand His nature and their calling. Disciples learn from their teacher to follow him. You cannot learn from Christ and walk in His footsteps without knowing the joy of serving (Mark 10:45).

Even a brief examination of Jesus' life reveals that He was a servant above all. Consider these facts. Jesus left heaven to live a life of poverty and pain on earth. Freed from the pursuit of pleasure and material things, Jesus spent His waking hours teaching, healing and encouraging others. For His kindness, He was criticized by jealous people who ridiculed and threatened Him. Despite nonstop opposition, Jesus continued to help people. He fed the hungry, tended the sick, comforted the bereaved, and taught the erring. For doing good, His enemies plotted to take His life. Jesus knew the end would not be quick and painless, but the certainty of torture could not deter Him from a life of ministry to those in need.

Jesus saw Himself as a servant. In Mark 10:45, He stated, "For even the Son of Man did not come to be served, but to serve, and to give his life a ransom for many." Service was not an isolated part of Jesus' life; rather, it defined His life. It was His identity, not merely a duty. If Jesus came to bring abundant life (John 10:10) and if He was a servant above all, then fullness of life must be equal to your growth as a servant. The more you give, the better you live. So deny yourself, take up your cross, and give yourself away in small deeds of love.

Welcome to the Christian Life

The gospel calls men and women to a lifetime of service as well as to forgiveness. Few are willing to dedicate their lives to Christ when they learn what is expected of them and what those who sacrifice so much can expect from others. For inconveniencing yourself and giving up your time or money, you get the satisfaction of helping a fellow traveler on his journey through life. However, doing good does not guarantee you will be appreciated. Occasionally, you will be judged, criticized and attacked, but what else would you expect? The same devil that opposed Christ will oppose anyone who serves in His name.

After hearing what Jesus demanded, many chose to walk away. To hold on to their money, comfort or pride, they parted company with the Lord. They were not prepared to change and grow – and that is exactly what service does. It challenges your view of life. It gives you a new perspective on what is truly valuable and important.

Are you prepared to lay down your life and take up your cross? Are you ready to be harassed for helping someone in need? Then welcome to the Christian life. Now you are set to grow by giving yourself away one word, one deed, one smile, one tear and one day at a time.

Growing Through Serving

But what does service have to do with growth? The natural course of life provides the answer. In the beginning, you come into the world without a care. Ideally, everything is provided by a loving mother and father who respond to your inarticulate needs. As you get older, some of the responsibility for your care is redirected to you. Perhaps you make up your bed, put your clothes in the hamper, and pick up your toys. As time goes on, you are asked to contribute to the family by helping out around the house. In addition to picking up after yourself, you set the table, wash dishes, take out the trash, mow the yard, or feed the pet.

Eventually you may choose to get married and care for the needs of another human being. It is a big jump from carefree college days to coordinating busy schedules and divvying up household chores, but this is part of growing up. Next, you enroll in the graduate school of serving called parenthood. Nothing teaches you to stretch and sacrifice like having children, yet the healthy and mature person thrives on this additional responsibility. The immature person avoids responsibility like the plague and resents what life requires of him. He expects others to do what he is not willing to do for himself. He believes wisdom is figuring out how to get others to carry his load in life. Consequently, his goal is to become sneakier rather than holier.

If you think joy is doing as little as possible, then you will know little joy in this life. Those who live for weekends and vacations pass the majority of their days unhappily. But if joy is relieving suffering, dispensing hope and helping people live better, then there are unlimited prospects for joy every day. Christians embrace these moments because of their faith and values. The key to multiplying your joy is simple: See service through Jesus' eyes.

Service helps you grow by enlarging your heart. It broadens your vision as you begin to notice other people and care about their struggles. It increases your discipline as you deny yourself to help someone in need. Amusements, pastimes and hobbies are put on hold to make room for higher priorities. To discern what is really important, you must appreciate what is truly valuable.

The ability to assess what matters is critical to the growth process. When your heart grows bigger; your vision, wider; your discipline, stronger; and your judgment, sharper, you enjoy a more abundant life. Undoubtedly, service is about furthering your growth as well as fulfilling another's needs.

Principles of Christian Service

(1) **Remember that sooner or later, you will need help too (Matthew 7:12).** George Washington Carver, an American inventor, said: "How far you go in life depends on your being tender with the young, compassionate with the aged, sympathetic with the striving and tolerant of the weak and strong. Because someday in your life you will have been all of these."

(2) **You do not have to be rich or famous to excel in giving (Matthew 10:42).** Jesus taught His disciples to practice serving in small ways. He praised the widow's two mites (Luke 21:1-3), promised rewards for a cup of water (Mark 9:41), and personally demonstrated how to wash feet (John 13:4-5). Serving is not about how much money you have in the bank but how much love you have in your heart.

(3) **You must open your eyes to see opportunities (John 4:35).** Wherever you find people, you find needs, and there are many people out there. Jesus said the fields "are already white for harvest!" In other words, there is plenty to do if you care enough to notice. The rich man ignored the beggar Lazarus at his gate because he was preoccupied with himself (Luke 16:19-21). Slow down, and take another look. You will be amazed by what you see.

(4) **Serving others is the reason you exist (Ephesians 2:10).** Every person was created with a unique talent and a common purpose. The purpose of life is to glorify God through loving words and deeds (Matthew 5:16). Because you entered the world with nothing and can take nothing out, the only way to be truly rich is to fulfill your purpose. That is what it means to lay up treasure in heaven (6:19-20). Have you made a deposit today?

(5) **God lets you choose between a life of selfishness or service (Romans 2:6-8).** Jesus did not stop the rich young ruler from walking away, but He did extend an invitation to a better life

(Matthew 19:16-22). The same choice is yours. Will you trust in Christ and share His joy of serving, or will you live for yourself and the moment? Living to serve is choosing to live.

(6) **The size of a deed does not determine its worth (Luke 17:6).** The value of a good deed cannot be printed out on your credit card statement. Small deeds can melt hearts and lift spirits. Never underestimate the value of timely words and deeds (Proverbs 25:11). True riches are measured in kindness, not karats.

(7) **Service is the truest expression of love (1 John 3:18).** John said, "Let us not love in word or in tongue, but in deed and in truth." Love is about your actions, not just your emotions. What you practice carries more weight than what you profess. So while good intentions are important, good works will always be the supreme expression of love.

(8) **You can make the world a better place (Matthew 25:34-36).** Most people undervalue how they contribute to others' lives. What seems routine to you may be unforgettable to a person in need. Just think: A simple meal, a little water, a brief visit, a change of clothes, a warm bed, or a bit of nursing are the things Jesus praised when contemplating the day of judgment. What do they have in common? They are everyday actions of caring people. What pleases God most is the tenderness of your heart, not the size of your talent.

(9) **You are more blessed by giving than receiving (Acts 20:35).** Being served relieves you, but serving others improves you. "More blessed" is the way Jesus described a life of service. "More" means greater by comparison, and "blessed" refers to a state of bliss and well-being. Do not settle for scraps of happiness. You always come out on top by putting others above yourself.

Leave Traces of Love

Some leave their mark on statues and stones. American sculptor Augustus Saint-Gaudens preserved the memory of the Civil War in his renderings of Colonel Robert Gould Shaw, General John A. Logan, and General William Tecumseh Sherman. At Stone Mountain, Ga., the likenesses of Jefferson Davis, Stonewall Jackson, and Robert E. Lee are carved in granite. But what of the soldiers of Christ? Where will their images be inscribed?

At Mount Sinai, the Lord wrote on stone tablets, but now He writes on hearts (Hebrews 8:10). Maybe we should too. Every time you serve others, you etch the gospel in their hearts and leave behind traces of your love. Upon whom will you write the story of Jesus today?

Questions

1. What do the penalties of sin teach us?

2. Why did Jesus say He came to earth (Mark 10:45)?

3. What can those who do Christ's work expect?

4. What did many do after learning Jesus' demands?

5. What is abundant life proportionate with?

6. Wherever you find people, what else will you find?

7. What is the only way to be truly rich?

8. How can you always come out on top?

9. If being served relieves you, what does serving others do for you?

10. Where did God choose to leave His mark?

For Discussion

1. What does service have to do with growth?

2. Why do some people avoid serving?

3. Where will you write your life's story?

Play of the Day

Ask your church secretary, if you have one, for the name and contact information of a newcomer to your congregation. Arrange a night to drop in for a brief visit, and let that person (or family) know you are bringing dessert (check on dietary restrictions). Carry paper plates, disposable utensils, paper cups, napkins and a plastic bag for hauling away the trash. Ask yourself what you would like to know if you were new to the congregation, and then put together a welcoming kit as a gift. Before leaving, say you would like to know one thing you could do to help make that person's transition easier. Do not take no for an answer. Keep asking, and offer suggestions. Once you get an answer, make it your top priority to get it done.

Welcoming Kit Suggestions
- Map of the church building.
- List of available Bible classes.
- Photo directory of church members.
- Office hours and phone numbers for the church.
- Church calendar.
- Edible treats.
- Community information.

Growth Strategy #8
Giving

"I want to be remembered as the guy who gave his all whenever he was on the field."
– Walter Payton, Running Back, Chicago Bears

Giving and growing go hand in hand. When done correctly, giving does more good for the benefactor than the beneficiary. The key is to follow the guidelines laid down in God's Word. By helping those in need, God also supplies your need. No one can follow the Bible's rules for giving without receiving more in return. Are you up for the challenge? Practice these 10 rules, and experience stewardship's amazing power to spark spiritual growth.

10 Rules for Giving

Rule 1: Give Purposely

> "So let each one give as he purposes in his heart"
> (2 Corinthians 9:7).

Giving as an afterthought does nothing to enlarge your soul. It is driven more by guilt than by faith or compassion. Its goal is relief rather than mercy. It aims to quiet your conscience and avoid embarrassment. Giving purposely has a higher motivation and produces better results. The kind of giving God wants requires forethought. It is a decision, not just a reaction. To give purposely means planning your giving.

At the beginning of the year, purpose how much you will increase your giving. Unless you are on a fixed income or have suffered a reversal at work, your contributions should increase over time. At the beginning of each month, make out your checks so that the money is not used for other things. By laying the money aside ahead of time, you accomplish two things: You reinforce your priorities and prepare yourself to live within your means. Without a clear decision, there can be no discipline.

Question to self: Do I plan my giving, or is it an afterthought (Proverbs 3:9-10)?

Rule 2: Give Proportionately

> "Let each one of you lay something aside, storing up as he may prosper" (1 Corinthians 16:2).

Few things bring more glory to God than generous giving. That is because stewardship is, above all, an expression of gratitude for His blessings. In a sense, your giving should be measured against God's giving. The more blessed you feel, the more bountiful your gifts will be. So how prosperous do you feel? As a Christian, do you feel less prosperous than Jews under the Law of Moses who gave a minimum of 10 percent of their income to the Lord? Do you feel less prosperous than those who lived in the humble circumstances of antiquity?

If you live in America, you are among the richest inhabitants on earth. Sadly, studies have revealed that the more affluent a person is, the less he gives in proportion to his total income. The amount may be great, but the sacrifice is small. Ironically, it is possible for greed to grow as your giving goes up. When increases in discretionary income outpace increases in your weekly contribution, you are falling behind spiritually.

Question to self: Is giving 10 percent my highest aspiration? Why not 25 percent or 50 percent (Luke 19:8)?

Rule 3: Give Cheerfully

"God loves a cheerful giver" (2 Corinthians 9:7).

Few things please God more than cheerful giving. Why does He delight in a positive disposition? Because no one can be happy in parting with money unless he shares God's values and appreciates His purpose. Cheerful giving is a measure of faith and love. Those who believe in heaven are more eager to give than those whose hopes are confined to this world. Those who care about people take more pleasure in giving than those who are self-absorbed. If you feel a twinge of regret when putting your money in the collection plate, it is a sign that growth is needed. If you feel irritated when your minister preaches on giving, it is a signal that something is wrong.

How you give has always been more important than the amount you give. Ananias and Sapphira were not punished because their gift was puny but because their hearts were greedy. The problem was they misrepresented it to impress others. Lying about their gift exposed their true motives. They were attempting to buy a reputation at a discount. Concern for the church was secondary.

Why should you be glad when you give? Because giving is a chance to glorify God. Because every dollar is a real blessing to someone in need. Because God has honored you to be part of the most important work in the world. Last but not least, because cheerful giving is an effective means of spiritual growth.

Question to self: Have I missed out on true joy by trying to buy earthly joy (1 John 2:15-17)?

Rule 4: Give Confidently

"And try Me now in this, Says the LORD of hosts" (Malachi 3:10).

At the O.K. Corral, Wyatt Earp had a showdown with the Clantons and McLaurys. The time had come for boastful lawbreakers to put up or shut up. When the collection plate passes today, it is a showdown for your heart. You are being called out by God. He challenges you to put His Word to the test, and He demands that the robbing come to an end (Malachi 3:8). In Malachi, Jews were called thieves for giving anything short of 10 percent. When Christians give 3 percent of their income and then brag about their faith in God and love for the lost, the Lord is not buying it.

It is time to get honest and get right. Even if you give twice as much as the average, you cannot boast in this. You may be robbing God less than worse offenders (only 4 percent rather than 7 percent), but you are robbing God nonetheless. Saints are not commanded to tithe, but it is hard to believe God would expect less of Christians than He expected of the Israelites. Why would God lower His expectations for earth's all-time richest residents? Malachi believed the problem behind stinginess was lack of faith. Those who trust God are more confident and aggressive in their giving. Be certain of this: He will never leave you, forsake you or shortchange you.

Question to self: Am I letting fear of the future keep me from giving what I could today?

Rule 5: Give Selflessly

> "But love your enemies, do good, and lend, hoping for nothing in return" (Luke 6:35).

In one of the great paradoxes in Scripture, Jesus taught His followers to give expecting nothing in return, but then added, "Your reward will be great" (Luke 6:35). The law of sowing and reaping cannot be broken, but the harvest is not restricted to this life. Selfless givers look to heaven for their reward, and pleasing God is their highest motive. Giving that God approves is driven by grace rather than greed and is merciful rather than mercenary. So when your generosity is not appreciated or reciprocated, do not let your heart grow cold. Blessings are on the way.

Question to self: Do I sometimes hesitate to give because I think it will be unappreciated?

Rule 6: Give Abundantly

> "He who sows bountifully will also reap bountifully" (2 Corinthians 9:6).

According to God's law, no one can give without receiving in return. Sparse giving is shortsighted because it limits what you can receive from the Lord. Bountiful giving is farsighted because it maximizes spiritual returns. Think of a company that matches a percentage of employee savings. The less workers give, the less they receive. On top of that, consider the benefits of compounded interest. Those who forego spending now to secure their futures will find their sacrifice rewarded exponentially. The secret to receiving more is giving more. If you want more joy, more self-respect, more peace of mind, and more goodwill on earth, then increase your giving until it hurts you without harming your family. Jeopardizing your solvency is ill-advised (because it can make you a burden to others). Challenging your complacency is spiritually astute.

Question to self: If my giving has plateaued, is it because of financial limits or faith limits?

Rule 7: Give Faithfully

> "On the first day of the week let each one of you lay something aside" (1 Corinthians 16:2).

Sporadic giving has more to do with your moods than your circumstances. Consistent giving is a sign of spiritual maturity and stability. Every Sunday, God gives you the opportunity to support the work of His kingdom. When you understand what a privilege this is, you never want to miss an opportunity. Your income may fluctuate, but your heart should remain steady.

You cannot give what you do not have, but do give something.

Consistent giving is more about your faith than your finances. So do not let fixed incomes, self-employment or seasonal sales become an excuse for irregularity. Just do what you can for the present, and position yourself to do more in the future. Constancy is the key to spiritual growth, so cultivate habits that move you in the direction of your goal. Make your giving an expression of commitment rather than convenience.

Question to self: Do I justify doing nothing because I cannot do as much as I would like?

Rule 8: Give Sacrificially

> "Their deep poverty abounded in the riches of their liberality" (2 Corinthians 8:2).

The Bible spotlights sacrificial givers to inspire you to imitate their devotion to God's kingdom. Barnabas liquidated his property to assist the infant church (Acts 4:35-37). A widow was celebrated for parting with her last two mites (Luke 21:1-3). The Macedonians demanded to participate in a special collection despite their deep poverty and affliction (2 Corinthians 8:1-2).

So what about you? Are you a sacrificial giver? Are you living above your means or giving above your means? Healthy sacrifice involves temporary loss for future gain. It is pain with a purpose. In a positive sense, it means giving up something of lesser value to obtain something of greater value. Purposeful sacrifice is the path to abundant life. Without sacrifice, the most you can hope for is an average life. The saying is true: You must give up to go up.

Question to self: Based solely on my giving, is my heart more in heaven or on earth (Matthew 6:21)?

Rule 9: Give Diversely

> "You pay tithe of mint and anise and cummin, and have neglected the weightier matters" (Matthew 23:23).

You cannot please God by substituting one Christian obligation for another: Service cannot take the place of giving, but neither can giving replace serving. Spiritual maturity is the result of balanced growth. The focus of this chapter is on becoming more intentional and joyful in your giving, but a warning is in order: It is possible to excel in giving yet be unpleasing to God.

When your spirit is right, generosity reaches beyond your wallet or purse. Liberality is the reflex of a grateful heart, and that holy impulse cannot be contained to one 5-minute portion of a weekly assembly. The desire to give should continue after the plate is passed and the congregation is dismissed. Healthy giving does not show up only on ledgers. It is about blessing lives, not just balancing budgets. Give generously, but never forget that loving actions are part of a diversified portfolio that pleases God.

Question to self: Am I limiting my growth by trying to substitute serving for giving or vice versa?

Rule 10: Give Spontaneously

"And when he saw him, he had compassion"
(Luke 10:33).

Becoming a disciplined, purposeful giver is a great goal, but it should not replace spontaneous acts of charity. Be sure to leave enough room in your budget so you can take advantage of unexpected opportunities to help your fellow man. If your budget is too tight, it takes away your options and more than a little joy. It will leave you feeling more deprived than a chocoholic without enough change to buy a candy bar. If you know what it feels like to deny your taste buds, imagine what it feels like to deny your soul's longings. Suffice it to say, it does not feel good when you want to give and cannot do so because you have not positioned yourself to be ready.

In a way, spontaneous giving really isn't so spontaneous after all. You cannot foresee the specific need, but you can anticipate there will be a need. It takes a great deal of planning to be able to assist when unplanned opportunities arise. You have to live beneath your means, have liquid assets available, and be alert to opportunities. If all of your giving is structured, you learn to ignore your heart's promptings. Your conscience grows numb and unfeeling. Benevolence becomes a weekly entry in your checkbook rather than a human event.

Question to self: Do I neglect opportunities to do good because I think giving on the Lord's Day is good enough?

A Parable on Giving

Once there was a small congregation whose members pledged to follow Jesus by obeying all of His teaching. One by one, they learned His instructions and kept them faithfully. Then one day, they noticed a command they had overlooked. They were studying Paul's writings and came across this passage about giving:

> But this I say: He who sows sparingly will also reap sparingly, and he who sows bountifully will also reap bountifully. So let each one give as he purposes in his heart, not grudgingly or of necessity; for God loves a cheerful giver. And God is able to make all grace abound toward you, that you, always having all sufficiency in all things, may have an abundance for every good work. (2 Corinthians 9:6-8)

Everyone knew this command would be hard to follow, much harder than others. They had been giving, but no one could say he or she had given "bountifully." When they came together on the Lord's Day, everyone gave something, but in their hearts, they knew they had given sparingly. The first thing they did was to look up the word "bountiful" in the dictionary. It said things like "generous," "great in quantity," "abundant," "more than adequate," "oversufficient," "richly supplied," "plentiful," "lavish," and "overflowing." None could say those words described his giving.

When they did the math, they realized they were giving about 5 percent of their net income. Someone mentioned God's people in the Old Testament gave more than 10 percent of everything they had. Another person recalled that Malachi said those who give less are robbing God. They all agreed they should do better, but one brave soul asked what was on everyone's mind: "Are you sure we can do it?" Someone answered, "Paul said God will help us if we try." A voice from the crowd agreed: "Yes! Paul said God will make His grace abound to us so we can abound to every good work."

All they had to do was spend less on themselves. At their next Bible class, they read passages on giving and then broke into groups to discuss ways to spend less so they could give more. When they remembered their purpose, they found it could be fun to pass up a treat or a bargain. Week after week, the contribution rose until they were giving twice as much as before. Laying by in store became one of the most exciting moments in the whole worship service. In the past, it had been a boring routine. When you give sparingly, that's how it feels.

The members of the little church grew more in faith, hope and love that year than any other time in recent memory. Those who heard they doubled their giving praised God for their amazing generosity. Soon the little church became a larger church. The more they gave, the more their hearts were in heaven; the more their hearts were in heaven, the more they loved to share their faith. It made them sad to think about the way they used to give and the blessings they missed for so long.

People who came from nearby towns always asked the same question: "How did you do it?" The members of the now big church always gave the same answer: "All we did was trust and obey. You see, once you take God's Word seriously, wonderful things happen."

Giving and Growing

Giving is about honoring the Lord, relieving human suffering, and accomplishing godly goals. It is also about growing up. It is a divinely approved means of developing more awareness, compassion and discipline. If you resent sermons on stewardship and appeals to support good works, you are revealing more about yourself than you realize. Your sensitivity suggests you think giving is a burden rather than a joy. Your irritability says you are self-satisfied and do not want to change.

The touchier you are on this topic, the guiltier you feel underneath. Pushback is about protecting your aching ego, and anger is a measure of your shame. The argument you are having is with yourself. You are conflicted and fighting a losing battle with your conscience. To face these facts is to grow up. Your determination to excel in giving opens the door to more joy and self-improvement. In addition to doing good, you are becoming more like Christ.

The worst feeling a football player can have is getting to the locker room after a game knowing he did not give his best. So when death comes and you step off life's playing field, how will you feel? And how will you be remembered? As one who gave his all for Christ or as one who gave precious little? May your generosity abound to God's glory and inspire those who follow to leave it all on the field.

Questions

1. Name two things you accomplish by setting aside your contribution ahead of time.

2. How can giving more sometimes be less?

3. What is cheerful giving a measure of?

4. When is it a showdown for your heart?

5. What did Jesus promise if you give expecting nothing in return?

6. Why is sparse giving shortsighted?

7. Consistent giving is a sign of what?

8. Without sacrifice, what is the most you can hope for?

9. When faith is genuine, what happens after the offering plate is passed?

10. What can your weekly contribution never replace?

For Discussion

1. How might you train children to be generous in their giving?

2. If you decided to excel in giving, how would you go about it?

3. When you see God face to face, will you wish you gave more?

Play of the Day

Hold a family meeting to talk about the privilege of giving. If you are single, meet with a friend or elder. Review the rules in this chapter; then purpose what you will give starting next Sunday. Stretch yourself, but be sure what you commit to is sustainable. The critical thing is to get on a growth path and increase as you can. Make it a habit to write your contribution check first and to adjust as needed in other areas.

Growth Strategy #9
Evangelism

"It's okay to have personal ambitions, but you have to take someone with you."
– Roger Staubach, Quarterback, Dallas Cowboys

The area of a football field inside an opponents' 20-yard line is called the "red zone." Evangelism is the red zone of the Christian life, marked by the crimson blood of Jesus. When you share the story of His sacrificial death, you are treading on holy ground.

Of all the dreams that fill the hearts of Christ's disciples, saving a soul from hell tops the list. More than health, wealth or fame, Christians long for opportunities to share the gospel. And is it any surprise that evangelism provides amazing opportunities for your own spiritual growth? Sharing Christ increases your courage, conviction and compassion. As a result, it improves your quality of life. In addition to rescuing a lost soul, you revive your own.

Hitting Your Stride

You know you are hitting your stride in the growth zone when sharing the gospel becomes as natural as saying hello. There are situations where sharing the gospel can make you tense, but in most cases, it ought to occur spontaneously. Evangelism is the overflowing of a joyful heart, the natural result of falling in love with Jesus.

People love to talk about their favorite subjects. Ask them about their hobby or favorite vacation and then sit back and get ready to listen. Grandparents delight in telling you about their grandchildren. Give them the slightest opening, and stories, pictures and smiles will flow like a mountain stream in springtime. Or consider two sweethearts who have fallen in love. It takes little coaxing for them to tell you the virtues of their beloved. Words of adoration pour from their lips like water rushing over Niagara Falls. They cannot help themselves.

Evangelism is less about arm-twisting and debate tactics than automatic expressions of heartfelt praise. It is more instinctive than institutional and more reflexive than regimented. People naturally talk about what is on their minds. If your heart is filled with Christ, He will seep into your speech, ooze into your emails, trickle into your telephone calls, and creep into every corner of your life. Evangelism is about your cup running over: "For out of the abundance of the heart his mouth speaks" (Luke 6:45).

When you walk in the Spirit, evangelism becomes second nature. When you do not, it is unnatural and uncomfortable. By following the growth strategies outlined in this book, you will find yourself talking more and more about Jesus in your everyday conversations. Evangelism is not something extra you do; it is a natural part of all you do. If speaking Jesus' name makes you nervous, you may want to go back and check on how you are doing with the eight previous strategies. Let's do a quick review.

Commitment

Without a deep commitment to Christ, evangelism will be difficult if not impossible. Ask yourself, is my religion merely about avoiding punishment, or is it about embracing and honoring God's Son? Fear grabs your attention with its negative energy, but it can have a short motivational shelf life. Faith, hope and love are far more likely to sustain you over the long haul. They are renewable sources of spiritual energy that can make you a faithful finisher like Christ (John 19:30). No doubt, fear has its place, but love is the most powerful and positive force in the world. The former repels.

The latter attracts. So to keep the faith and share it effectively, you need more than dread. You need loving devotion to God's Son.

Fellowship

If you do not value the church, you will find it hard to win others to Christ. Why? Because the church is Jesus' body to which all saved people are added (Acts 2:47). If you cherish God's family, it will be evident in your words and tone. Ask yourself, do I see the church as a loving family or an outdated organization? Because Jesus purchased the church with His blood, fellowship must be the most precious thing on earth. The church of Christ is made up of imperfect people who love, forgive and support one another as they journey to heaven. Along the way, they help one another grow in Christlikeness and overcome worldliness. Loving elders, supportive assemblies and caring brethren are foundational to spiritual growth but also to evangelism.

Bible Study

If you are not spending time in the Word, you will lack the confidence it takes to talk about your faith. The gospel is "the power of God to salvation" (Romans 1:16), but you must know it to share it. If you neglect study, you may feel too weak to speak when opportunities arise. Every passage you treasure in your heart prepares you to connect with others who have the same needs and longings as you. It is not necessary to know everything before reaching out, but unless your heart is full of God's Word, you may hesitate when the moment arrives. Simply put, you cannot give what you do not have. Study equips you with knowledge and courage to engage others in conversation. That is why Paul commanded, "Be diligent to present yourself approved to God, a worker who does not need to be ashamed, rightly dividing the word of truth" (2 Timothy 2:15).

Prayer

If you are not praying, you will lack the sense of God's presence needed to venture beyond your comfort zone. When you feel close to God, you sense His power, which aids you in reaching out to others in His name. Paul prayed for courage to be bold in sharing the gospel (Ephesians 6:19-20). Through prayer, you can become more confident in sharing your faith. The less time you spend in prayer, the less mindful you are of evangelistic opportunities (John 4:35-36). When you pray more, you see more. When you pray less, you say less.

Discipline

If your life is out of control, you will not spend much time talking about Jesus because you will be embarrassed for people to know you are a Christian. Your behavior at the ballpark, office party, PTA meeting or workplace provides the context for your evangelistic efforts. Self-discipline increases your credibility and your eagerness to share what might otherwise be awkward to convey.

Virtue

Without virtue, you will lack the integrity and interpersonal skills needed to communicate the gospel effectively. That is why the fruit of the Spirit is critical to any relational undertaking. The basic element in evangelism is people. Sharing the gospel is a human enterprise requiring social skills refined by the Spirit of God. These qualities are taught at self-improvement seminars, but they are the natural tendencies of people who are filled with love for God and one another. Caring is the key to connecting, and that is why being filled with God's Spirit is fundamental to sharing your faith.

Service

Unless you are serving, you will lack the genuine concern for others that motivates people to share their faith. That is why empathy and evangelism are inseparable. Both are about caring for the needs of others. They are matters of the heart. If you will not relieve the hungry, sick or bereaved, whose needs are immediate and obvious, it is doubtful you will be concerned about something as seemingly remote as eternity. On the other hand, if you are sympathetic to someone's physical and emotional needs, your sympathy will prompt you to consider the greater needs of the soul. Service and evangelism are signs of spiritual health and growth. They are labors of love that require no repayment but the joy of doing good.

Giving

In the Sermon on the Mount, Jesus taught His disciples the importance of stewardship with these words:

> Do not lay up for yourselves treasures on earth, where moth and rust destroy and where thieves break in and steal; but lay up for yourselves treasures in heaven, where neither moth nor rust destroys and where thieves do not break in and steal. For where your treasure is, there your heart will be also. (Matthew 6:19-21)

If you are not giving generously and cheerfully, your heart is not in heaven. If your heart is not in heaven, how could you possibly convince anyone else to go there? Empty plate, empty heart, empty words.

Perseverance

The next chapter of this book will introduce you to perseverance as the final strategy in God's game plan for spiritual growth. Perseverance is fundamental to achieving goals, and evangelism is no exception. Jesus' enduring love led to unmatched success in seeking and saving the lost. If not for this holy resolve, He would have cut His mission short and returned to heaven. Similarly, effective evangelists face many frustrations, but they do not give up easily. They are dogged and resolute. Their endurance can be attributed to two things: love for the lost and gratitude for the One who did not give up on them. Divine love is unrelenting, and those who have tasted it develop a Christlike tenacity for recovering lost souls.

A Simple Plan

Did you know most people attending a worship service are not there because of the preacher? They are there because someone cared enough to invite them. Evangelism is much simpler than you think. It basically comes down to caring and sharing. When was the last time you

- Invited someone to worship with you?
- Asked someone about her faith and listened before responding?
- Told someone how Jesus and His church have blessed your life?

If you are not recruiting people to God's team, two possible reasons are you have quit growing and are just going through the motions or you have fallen out of love with Jesus but don't have the courage or honesty to call it quits. When the Ephesian church let their love grow cold, Jesus told them there was an alternative to passionless religion (Revelation 2:1-7). To find their way back to Him, two things were necessary: They must do the first works, and they must remember from where they had fallen. If your religious experience feels like being trapped in a loveless marriage, then consider how Jesus' advice can revive your faith and fervor.

• **"Do the first works."** In other words, get back to basics. How? By rededicating yourself to the growth strategies in this book: Renew your commitment to Christ; spend more time in fellowship with His people; study more; pray without ceasing; increase your self-control; develop more virtue; find a place to serve; and give more than you have in the past. By recommitting yourself to these fundamentals, you will spark a spiritual revival in your life that will overflow into the lives of others.

• **"Remember from where [you have] fallen."** Do you recall what it was like to be lost and how good it felt when your sins were washed away? Remember the joy Jesus brought you before you started taking Him for granted and let the world come between you. Too many married couples let the busyness of life rob them of the joy they shared in their earlier years. The same thing can happen in your relationship with Christ. Love warms the heart like a fire, but you must fan the flames. When the embers of spiritual devotion grow cold, Jesus says: "Don't give up on us. Let me remind you of what we could be." It is never too late for love.

By heeding these instructions, you can revive your devotion to Christ and your desire to reach lost souls. The closer you are to Jesus, the more natural evangelism will become. And the more you share your faith, the more you will flourish spiritually. To reach full maturity as a Christian, you must love souls and live for heaven above all else. That is why sharing the gospel is the supreme strategy for spiritual growth.

Questions

1. What is the "red zone" of the Christian life?

2. How do you know that church fellowship is precious?

3. If you are not spending time in God's Word, what will you lack in regard to evangelism?

4. When you pray less, what will happen in regard to evangelism?

5. What gives an evangelist credibility?

6. What gives you the interpersonal skills you need to share the gospel?

7. If you are not serving, what will you lack as an evangelist?

8. If you are not giving cheerfully and generously, what does that indicate? What impact does that make on your evangelistic efforts?

9. What is the crowning condition of effective evangelism?

10. Why do most first-time visitors attend a worship service?

For Discussion

1. How does sharing your faith promote spiritual growth?

2. What is the hardest part of evangelism for you?

3. How could evangelism become a more natural part of your life?

Play of the Day

For the next week, begin each day by asking God to help you spot an opening for sharing Jesus with someone who needs Him. Also pray for the courage to speak when the moment presents itself. Do not judge your success by the immediate result of the conversation. Your job is to plant the seed. If the hearer's heart is good and noble, the harvest will come in due season.

Growth Strategy #10
Perseverance

"God places the heaviest burden on those who can carry its weight."
– Reggie White, Defensive End, Philadelphia Eagles

I n football, the last 10 yards are nearly always the toughest. The field of play shrinks to the advantage of the defense. The opponent digs in with bulldog determination. The noise becomes deafening. On top of it all, exhaustion creeps into every cell of the athlete's body, taunting him and tempting him to settle for less than his best effort. As the fourth quarter draws to a close, the long march down the field takes its toll. Aching muscles begin to cramp, and weary minds begin to waver. Vince Lombardi, Green Bay Packers coach, said it well: "Fatigue makes cowards of us all."

In the final minutes of a game, a team shows what it is really made of. Each player's courage and commitment are tested. All that has gone before will be for naught without the ability to finish well. So it is with the Christian life. To stop short of the goal is unthinkable. Heaven is not for the shortsighted or half-hearted. Although salvation does not hinge on heroic human effort, it does hang on one humble but essential virtue: endurance. There is one thing every person will share in common in glory: They did not quit.

Paul's Threefold Challenge

In a close game, when everything is on the line, when there is
no tomorrow, when momentum is slipping away and the team's
strength and confidence with it, it is the coach's job to rally the
spirits of his players. Good coaches know success is a state of
mind. Attitude cannot take the place of conditioning, strategy
or practice, but all things being equal, it is the difference maker.
That is why Paul offered these words to battle-weary believers:

> Therefore, my beloved brethren, be steadfast, im-
> movable, always abounding in the work of the Lord,
> knowing that your labor is not in vain in the Lord.
> (1 Corinthians 15:58)

1. Be Steadfast

Near the close of Paul's first letter to the Corinthians, he issued
an urgent plea for renewed dedication. The struggling congregation had many problems, but throwing in the towel would not
improve any of them. Paul did not offer quick fixes and easy solutions for the difficulties they faced. What they needed was more
love and lots of grit. Grit is the extreme determination that grows
from love, and lasting change is not possible without it.

Paul's plea for perseverance corresponds to the resolute
nature of God. You do not have to wonder about God's
mood on any particular day. Every morning, a fresh supply
of mercy awaits you:

> Through the LORD's mercies we are not consumed,
> because his compassions fail not. They are new every
> morning; great is Your faithfulness. "The LORD is my
> portion," says my soul, "Therefore I hope in Him!"
> (Lamentations 3:22-24)

God's goodness is more certain than tomorrow's sunrise. No
temporary blackout will ever occur – not for one day, one hour
or one second. Faithful, reliable and consistent mercy is His
gift. The Maker of heavenly light shines His grace on you with a

dependability surpassing the circuit of the sun, the orbit of the moon, or the constancy of the stars (James 1:17).

God's love can never change because it is His essence. Pretending to be something you are not is exhausting. God is no pretender. He is not an aspiring deity at work on the rough edges of pseudo-perfection. God is love. Therefore, He cannot be anything less – ever. Although Christians are imperfect, they seek to emulate God's love to the fullest extent possible. That means becoming a loving person at the core of your being. It also means loving unconditionally, regardless of your moods or circumstances.

To be steadfast you must develop a consistent loving nature. Most people are caring from time to time, but Christians are called to display a more perfect and persistent love. They do this by following the example of God's Son (John 13:15). To be like Jesus, you cannot place limits on your love. When betrayed, cursed, slandered, abused or persecuted, you must not respond in kind (Matthew 5:43-48). These things will happen repeatedly in your lifetime, so choosing to retaliate is sentencing yourself to unending hostility. By forbearing and forgiving, your spirit will be lighter; your health, better; and your relationships, closer. It is the only sensible and decent way to live.

Four Foundations for a Faithful Life

The Bible highlights four areas where steadfastness is needed to live a more caring and responsible life. After the establishment of Jesus' church on Pentecost, Luke recorded these words about early Christians: "And they continued steadfastly in the apostles' doctrine and fellowship, in the breaking of bread, and in prayers" (Acts 2:42). These four practices are foundational for sustaining spiritual growth and relating effectively.

(1) Study: God's Word teaches people how to grow spiritually and love genuinely. That is why Bible study is so important. Knowledge does not guarantee growth, but it does facilitate growth.

Luke's emphasis on "continuing steadfastly" (Acts 2:42) in the apostle's doctrine suggests there is a relationship between regular study and spiritual growth. Occasional contact with Scripture cannot have the same effect as consistent contact with God's Word. Those who develop the discipline of daily Bible study are blessed by the cumulative knowledge they develop over time.

However, there is something to be said for just being in touch with God through His written Word. It is not merely the depth and breadth of your biblical knowledge that matters. It is the orientation of your heart toward God. Factual knowledge must be completed by personal knowledge of God. Bible study is about relationship, not just regulations.

It has been said: "Love is like playing the piano. First you must learn to play by the rules; then you must forget the rules and play from your heart." In truth, the rules are not forgotten but learned so well they are held more deeply in the subconscious mind. Actions that once required conscious effort have become second nature to a heart long-immersed in God's Word and ways (Jeremiah 31:33; Hebrews 8:10).

Still, a warning is in order. The desire for intimacy with God should never become an excuse for ignoring the details of divine revelation. Minimizing doctrinal correctness in the name of closeness is a tactic of false teachers. Truth and intimacy are complementary in healthy relationships.

Finally, Luke's exhortation should not be limited to study alone. Continuing in the apostles' doctrine includes the idea of conforming your life to their instruction. It speaks of a deep commitment to lifelong learning and continual improvement in Christian living.

(2) Fellowship: To enjoy nonstop growth, you need friends and supporters equally committed to growth. That is why Paul warned against intimate friendships with nonbelievers (1 Corinthians 15:33; 2 Corinthians 6:14-17). Church assemblies bring you in contact with those who share the vision and values of Christ. That is what fellowship is all about. If I am lacking in faith, hope or love, where do I get it? I cannot give myself what I do not have. In the give and take of fellowship, Christians are equipped and encouraged to carry on the work of Jesus.

Fellowship refers to partnership. Partners are people who labor together to accomplish a common goal. They combine their intellects, energy and resources to achieve what none could do alone. They support one another's efforts and sustain one another's spirits. Christians are partners in Christ's work of freeing people from sin to enjoy abundant life in God's kingdom. No earthly association can compare with the camaraderie of those whose purpose is to live and love like Jesus.

(3) Communion: Athletes are frequently required to eat meals together. They gather around the training table not only to ensure good nutrition but to bond as a team. Jesus understood the benefits of sharing food to build closeness among His followers and instituted a weekly meal with mandatory attendance. This event is referred to as breaking bread because bread is the first of two courses in this spiritual feast. It is hard to overestimate the importance of being around the Lord's Table on the first day of the week. Both Scripture and history attest to the regularity of this practice by early Christians.

Partaking of Christ's body and blood strengthens you to go the second mile in spreading the gospel and serving your fellow man. It is not the dietary value of the meal that matters. Rather, you are spiritually revived by feeding your mind on Jesus' death, burial and resurrection. Recalling His love awakens your soul and reconnects you to His body. It challenges you to rise above the selfishness that destroys relationships.

Participants in the Lord's Supper focus their minds on two aspects of Christ's work: one from the past and one promised for the future. The crucifixion is the first aspect. Christians must never forget how much Jesus suffered to forgive their sins. His death reveals the sacrificial nature of love and provides a pattern for His disciples to follow.

Next comes the promise of a wondrous event yet to occur: Christ's second coming. This promise is a reminder that you are on His mind. Do not forget Him, because He has not forgotten you. Like family members who anxiously await a holiday gathering, Christ longs to be in your presence as much as you yearn to be in His.

(4) Prayer: Luke's fourth foundation for a faithful life is persistent prayer. Each item on the apostle's list is designed to produce staying power in the face of life's challenges.

- The Bible transforms the mind.
- Fellowship encourages the heart.
- The Lord's Supper centers the soul.
- Prayer reinforces the will.

Prayer is the sturdy string that ties this entire bundle of God's blessings into a complete package. A Bible is not always handy, fellowship may not be available, and the Lord's Supper may be six days away, but prayer is always a possibility. The accessibility of prayer makes it crucial for living a faithful life. Yet because of its convenience, it is often overlooked. Perhaps that is why Luke closed by reminding readers that devoted Christians of earlier days continued steadfastly in prayer. The first and last items on a list carry special importance because their placement makes them easier to remember. Prayer is the exclamation point of Luke's fourfold plea for faithfulness. If you hope to endure, by all means pray (Luke 18:1).

Prayer promotes endurance by reconnecting you with the benefits of the other disciplines. It enhances the blessings of study, fellowship and communion by releasing their power stored in your memory. Prayer links you with His Word, His people and His sacrifice.

Most of all, prayer is essential to endurance because it is a continual link to love. How many times have you heard a prayer leader give thanks for God's love or ask for help to love more like Christ? Prayer produces spiritual resilience by reinforcing your will to love better. As a recipient of divine love, it is your duty to share what you have received. Prayer strengthens that desire.

2. Be Immovable

The J.B. Phillips Version of 1 Corinthians 13:7-8 reads: "Love knows no limit to its endurance, no end to its trust, no fading of its hope; it can outlast anything. It is, in fact, the one thing that still stands when all else has fallen." In other words, love is the stabilizing force of life. It makes you steady in times of uncertainty and adversity.

Sturdy love is essential for winning life's battles. Paul wrote, "Therefore take up the whole armor of God, that you may be able to withstand in the evil day, and having done all, to stand" (Ephesians 6:13). To withstand means to hold your ground. At the end of the day, you have not been defeated nor have you retreated.

The armor of God refers to the mental reinforcement of loving thoughts. The more you love God and care about others, the less erratic your behavior. Love makes you predictable in good ways. Your family and friends know they can count on you to help rather than harm them. Your consistency makes you trustworthy and battleworthy.

The individual pieces of armor describe the attitudes and actions that grow out of a loving mindset. Loving people are dependable in speaking the truth, standing up for right, and promoting peace. They are immovable in doing good because of faith in God's Word and His promises (Ephesians 6:14-17).

3. Abound in the Work of the Lord

The apostle's third charge was to abound in the work of the Lord. That means living defensively is not enough to produce abundant life. The goal of Christianity is not merely to hang on until Christ returns. It is to glorify God by saving souls and doing good.

Have you ever watched a football game where a team with a slim lead stopped playing aggressively? Defenders dropped back to play prevent defense. Playing not to lose can have disastrous effects because it is foreign to an athlete's natural inclinations. It makes him tentative and throws off his timing. It also allows the opponent to dictate the terms of the game.

Something similar occurs when Christians become timid in living their faith. Paul understood that faithfulness to God is more than playing it safe while the clock runs out. Consequently, he refused to end his life trying to avoid personal loss. He lived and wrote and preached with passion until his dying day. He chose to live on offense.

Abundant life entails risk, and those who would live victoriously must abound in the work of the Lord. The word "abound" refers to plenty. It describes a life overflowing with love and goodness (1 Thessalonians 3:12-13; Philippians 1:9-11). Because God abounds in love for all mankind (Exodus 34:6; John 3:16), you do His work when you love people and care for their needs (1 John 3:18; 4:8). Paul was encouraging lavish acts of kindness, generosity and service.

Christians who give meagerly and serve reluctantly are kidding no one with their sparing displays of faith. Living not to go to hell is a recipe for spiritual disaster. It is driven by guilt rather than gratitude, and the difference is glaring. You cannot abound in the work of the Lord without loving Jesus more than self, heaven more than earth, and people more than pleasure. So based on your work for the Lord, are you playing offense or defense?

Now let's put all three of Paul's instructions together to see how they complement each other.

> **(1) Be Steadfast:** Don't resign.
> **(2) Be Immovable:** Don't retreat.
> **(3) Abound in the Work of the Lord:** Don't relax.

The abundant life is not for cowards or quitters. It is for those who endure and abound in the work of the Lord. So do not shirk your responsibility, shrink from opportunity, or settle for mediocrity. Victory belongs to those who face life's challenges with faith, hope and much love. That explains why Paul could "rejoice in the Lord" despite shipwreck and stoning (Philippians 4:4; 2 Corinthians 11:25); why he could sing of God's love from the stocks of a dreary prison (Acts 16:25); and why He could face death with an eagerness for eternity (2 Timothy 4:8). Quitting, cowering and coasting were never options for Paul.

If victory is about worldly pleasure, then Paul was a failure; but if it is about God's pleasure, then he was a genuine success. The more you love, give, serve and grow, the better life gets. So no matter what happens, do not

- Give up.
- Give ground.
- Give less than your best.

Questions

1. What will every person share in common in glory?

2. Name three things Paul commanded in 1 Corinthians 15:58.

3. Lasting change is not possible without what?

4. What is the primary way Christians should seek to be steadfast?

5. What are the four foundations of a steadfast life (Acts 2:42)?

6. What does it mean to "withstand" (Ephesians 6:13)?

7. What do the individual pieces of the armor of God represent (Ephesians 6:14-17)?

8. What is true manliness?

9. What does the word "abundance" mean?

10. What is the "work of the Lord" in which Christians should abound?

For Discussion

1. How would you describe a steadfast Christian life?

2. How can you use the armor of God to become immovable?

3. How can Christians abound in the work of the Lord?

Play of the Day

Perseverance is developed through practice. Think of one habit that will help you be a better Christian, and commit to practicing it consistently for the next year. Make a list of strategies that will help you follow through, and post them on your bathroom mirror. Share your goal with others, and pray about it daily. Enter the date on your calendar when you began trying to change the habit and one year later to assess your progress.

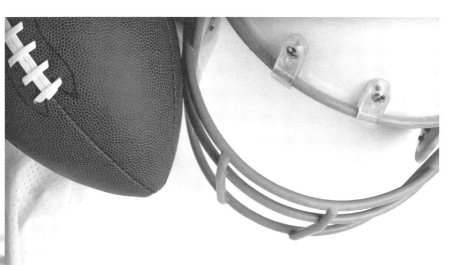

Postseason

Live
Eternally

"In my Father's house are many mansions;
if it were not so, I would have told you.
I go to prepare a place for you" (John 14:2).

Longing for
Heaven

**"If you're not going to go all the way,
why go at all?"**
– Joe Namath, Quarterback, New York Jets

W hen the regular season comes to a close, postseason
play is just beginning. The bowl season is what college
players dream about all year long – or their entire lives
long. The pageantry, glamour and hype are the stuff of young
people's fantasies. The point is it is on their minds most of the
time. During tryouts, practice, the season opener, and every game
to follow, visions of postseason play linger in the background.

Heaven is much like that. You do not stumble into heaven by
accident. You dream about it and live for it. Eternity should not
be an afterthought. Thoughts of your destiny should dictate your
decisions every day. No, glory cannot be earned through a stellar performance on earth's playing field. There are no Heisman
trophies in heaven, but a genuine life of faith is essential. In fact,
heaven is one gorgeous, state-of-the-art hall of faith.

Some parents hope their children will experience bowl glory.
Christian parents want their children to know eternal glory. Their
greatest desire is not for a smart, wealthy, talented or good-looking
child. Their highest hope is for their child to go to heaven. In
the end, though, every person must embrace this goal in his own
heart. To live in heaven, you must first long for heaven.

The Power of Anticipation

Looking forward to special events can be as much fun as the event itself (it certainly helps to fill the time while you are waiting). Children obsess about birthdays and holidays. Teenagers daydream about driver's licenses and first dates. Young adults spend enormous amounts of time planning their weddings and envisioning the perfect house. Middle-age couples save for world-class vacations and a comfortable retirement. In most cases, anticipation is half the fun. Thinking, talking, saving and preparing can be a delight, but occasionally, the big event does not live up to your expectations (think of your first kiss).

One things is for certain: Heaven will not be a disappointment. No one will say: "You mean this is it? That's all there is?" No one will be put to shame for hoping too much. Heaven will be both perfect and unending. Paul wrote to the Ephesians:

> Now to Him who is able to do exceedingly abundantly above all that we ask or think, according to the power that works in us, to Him be glory in the church by Christ Jesus to all generations, forever and ever. Amen. (Ephesians 3:20-21)

To put it plainly, heaven will surpass your wildest dreams. Or remember Paul's words to the Corinthians: "Eye has not seen, nor ear heard, nor have entered into the heart of man the things which God has prepared for those who love Him" (1 Corinthians 2:9). In addition to preparing a way of salvation, God is preparing a home for the saved that will exceed the highest expectations of its future residents.

Paul's Daily Challenge

Christians are encouraged to think about heaven on a daily basis (Titus 2:11-14). Contemplating heaven has a centering effect on the mind. It inspires holy living and healthy relationships. People who think a great deal about heaven live differently from those who do not. Understanding this, Paul urged:

> If then you were raised with Christ, seek those things
> which are above, where Christ is, sitting at the right hand
> of God. Set your mind on things above, not on things
> on the earth. For you died, and your life is hidden with
> Christ in God. When Christ who is our life appears, then
> you also will appear with Him in glory. (Colossians 3:1-4)

What are the "things above," which are worthy of your most
ardent affections? There are three heavenly realities that are
"above" and that must not be forgotten. "Above" is where Christ
is. Paul envisioned Jesus seated on His throne at the right
hand of our heavenly Father. Obviously then, "above" is where
God dwells. And finally, "above" is where glory is found. When
Christ returns, you will take full possession of eternal life as
your body is refitted to suit your perfected surroundings. That
will be glory indeed.

But in addition to anticipating these heavenly realities, saints
must center their minds on heavenly values. When you do this,
the results are practical and beneficial.

> Therefore put to death your members which are on
> the earth: fornication, uncleanness, passion, evil desire,
> and covetousness, which is idolatry. Because of these
> things the wrath of God is coming upon the sons of
> disobedience, in which you yourselves once walked
> when you lived in them. But now you yourselves are
> to put off all these: anger, wrath, malice, blasphemy,
> filthy language out of your mouth. Do not lie to one
> another, since you have put off the old man with his
> deeds. (Colossians 3:5-9)

Step one is putting away evil desires and the harmful behaviors
they produce. Paul urged a zero-tolerance policy in regard to worldly
ways: They must be put to death. Thanks to Christ, your past does
not have to be your future. To fortify your will, the apostle reminded
his readers that God's wrath will be poured out on those who yield
to sinful longings and settle down to lives of disobedience. Christians will not win every battle, but they can never give up the fight.

Step two is replacing old habits with better ones:

> Therefore, as the elect of God, holy and beloved, put
> on tender mercies, kindness, humility, meekness, long-
> suffering; bearing with one another, and forgiving one
> another, if anyone has a complaint against another;
> even as Christ forgave you, so you also must do. But
> above all these things put on love, which is the bond
> of perfection. And let the peace of God rule in your
> hearts, to which also you were called in one body; and
> be thankful. Let the word of Christ dwell in you richly
> in all wisdom, teaching and admonishing one another
> in psalms and hymns and spiritual songs, singing with
> grace in your hearts to the Lord. And whatever you
> do in word or deed, do all in the name of the Lord
> Jesus, giving thanks to God the Father through Him.
> (Colossians 3:12-17)

Depending on willpower to defeat sin is a losing proposition.
You must build positive habits to support your goals. Those habits
are rooted in a vision of the new person you want to become to
glorify God and do good in the world. Christians must set their
affections on things above because holy desires are roused by
heavenly aspirations. "Affections" are positive longings. To "set"
them means to fix them in your mind; to concentrate on them.

It is essential to warn people about hell (2 Corinthians 5:11;
Revelation 20:11-15), but it is far more important to remind them
about heaven. Nothing draws out human potential like contemplating eternal glory. If you lack spiritual drive, spend more time
pondering Christ's example, filling your heart with His words,
and imagining your home with Him in heaven.

Count Your Heavenly Blessings

So what are you most looking forward to in heaven? Is it the
beauty and plenty or the harmony of a realm where sin cannot
enter? Some things you will not be able to find in heaven. There
will be no screaming, lying, backbiting or gossiping in heaven.

In other words, there will be no physical or verbal abuse. Love and good will fill every nook and cranny of the New Jerusalem.

Perhaps there is someone special you will be looking for when you awake in heaven. I know my wife and I will no longer be married when we get there, but we look forward to hanging out together as eternal friends. We have agreed that when one of us passes, we will not let sorrow rob us of the true meaning of the moment. We have decided ahead of time to be happy for whoever gets to go to heaven first. That doesn't mean we won't have sad moments or shed tears. Sorrow is a measure of the value you place on what you have lost.

Paul said heavenly thoughts are comforting thoughts. Knowing the truth and believing God's promises set Christians apart from those who have no hope (1 Thessalonians 4:13-18). Heaven is about hope – not wishful thinking but absolute certainty that the best is yet to come. As a child, it is hard to be sad when thinking about birthday parties, dates and graduations. As God's child, it is impossible to grieve uncontrollably when envisioning illness-proof bodies, mortgage-free accommodations, and abuse-free relationships.

The splendor of heaven is multifaceted, but the thing I most look forward to is reunions with people I am temporarily separated from by death. From this side or the other, I will be watching for dear ones who trusted in Christ and lived for heaven. Margaret Widdemer's poem "The Watcher" captures the powerful emotions that sustain us till that time:

> She always leaned to watch for us,
>   Anxious if we were late,
> In winter by the window,
>   In summer by the gate;
>
> And though we mocked her tenderly,
>   Who had such foolish care,
> The long way home would seem more safe,
>   Because she waited there.

> Her thoughts were all so full of us,
>   She never could forget!
> And so I think that where she is
>   She must be watching yet,
>
> Waiting till we come home to her,
>   Anxious if we are late –
> Watching from Heaven's window,
>   Leaning from Heaven's gate.

The Ultimate Guessing Game

When waiting in airports, one of my favorite pastimes is to guess where people may be going. Is the man in uniform on his way to the battlefront or to a bear hug from his waiting family? Is the man in the Hawaiian shirt headed for a second honeymoon or for a golf vacation with buddies? People's dress and demeanor provide clues about where they are headed.

Have you ever seen someone you knew was headed for heaven? One thing is for sure: The disciples knew exactly where Jesus was headed (John 14:1-3). The thief on the cross had no confusion about Christ's ultimate destination (Luke 23:42-43). The centurion was confident the man he just executed was on His way home to God (vv. 46-47; Mark 15:39).

Similarly, it's likely no one who met Paul could have remained in doubt about where he was going. Why? Because he constantly talked about it. Churches and colleagues must have been encouraged by his confidence in a heavenly reward. Some doubted Paul's sanity (Acts 26:24), but they likely did not question his certainty. As you read Paul's letters, do you have any doubt about the consuming desire of his heart?

> For to me, to live is Christ, and to die is gain. But if I live on in the flesh, this will mean fruit from my labor; yet what I shall choose I cannot tell. For I am hard-pressed between the two, having a desire to depart and be with Christ, which is far better. (Philippians 1:21-23)

> For I am already being poured out as a drink offering, and the time of my departure is at hand. I have fought the good fight, I have finished the race, I have kept the faith. Finally, there is laid up for me the crown of righteousness, which the Lord, the righteous Judge, will give to me on that Day, and not to me only but also to all who have loved His appearing. (2 Timothy 4:6-8)

What about you? Do people know where you are headed? Your classmates? Your co-workers? Your children? To answer that question honestly, ask yourself this: Do I think much about heaven? Do I talk much about eternity? Do I live each day for glory?

Tickets Please

During the regular season, football fans often travel to games without purchasing advance tickets. They know plenty will be for sale outside the stadium. However, bowl tickets can be harder to come by. If you want to be sure to get in, you have to buy them in advance.

When it comes to your destiny, why chance it? To enter glory, you need a reservation. Unless your name is written in the Lamb's Book of Life, you will be turned away at the door. And rest assured, there will be no scalpers outside the gates of heaven.

No one arrives in heaven by accident or slips in secretly. As the saying goes, heaven is a prepared place for a prepared people. So are you living for eternity? Have you set your affections above? Is going to heaven the deepest desire of your heart? The simple truth is that you live for what you long for. May your postseason be the stuff of your dreams.

Questions

1. What should never be an afterthought?

2. To live in heaven, what must you do first?

3. What does "affection" mean (Colossians 3:2 KJV)?

4. What does "set" mean (Colossians 3:2)?

5. Name three things that are found "above."

6. What is more important than warning people about hell?

7. What kinds of thoughts are comforting?

8. What will you not find in heaven?

9. What sets Christians apart from those who have no hope?

10. How might people have known Paul was headed to heaven?

For Discussion

1. What are you most looking forward to about heaven?

2. Name a person you believe is headed for heaven. What makes you believe this?

3. How can you increase your longing for heaven?

Play of the Day

Think of someone living you would like to be with in heaven. Get out your stationery and write him (or her) a personal letter explaining all the reasons you are looking forward to eternity. Close the letter by explaining how much you would like him to be there with you to share in God's blessings. Mail the letter.

Be a
Team Player

**"You and I are players; God's our coach;
and we're playing the biggest game of all.
We have a loving God that made us.
We need to get on His team."**

– Joe Gibbs, Coach, Washington Redskins

God loves to work in teams. That is why He created families. The church is God's spiritual family, and no one can live victoriously without the support of this team. Jesus established His church in Jerusalem on the Day of Pentecost following His death, burial and resurrection (Acts 2). From there, His team spread throughout Judea and Samaria and into the uttermost parts of the earth (1:8).

Each local church is culturally distinct, but there are some ways all of them should be alike: The Great Commandment (i.e., Matthew 22:35-38) and the Great Commission (i.e., 28:18-20) are shared commitments of every faithful church. Biblical standards of morality are universal and nonnegotiable. Scripture is the ultimate authority in all matters of faith and religious practice. Healthy churches must behave like teams to accomplish what God intended.

The more institutional and bureaucratic a church becomes, the less it fits the New Testament model. Paul compared the church to a human body (1 Corinthians 12:12-31). His analogy emphasized the need for two things: coordination and consideration.

1. Coordination

Every member of the body is valuable, and when members work in harmony, life is more enjoyable. When members of Christ's body respect their God-given roles and fulfill their responsibilities, the church is strong and functional.

2. Consideration

When you get a splinter in your finger or a speck in your eye, your entire body sympathizes. When a member of Christ's body suffers from sin, it affects the whole group. Christians bear one another's burdens and gently restore the erring. Whatever the problem or pain, they work together to resolve it.

When churches do not function like bodies, families or close-knit teams, the problem is a shortage of love. When selfishness grows, serving dwindles. Big egos take the place of big hearts. Fear and control replace faith and trust, and jealousy triumphs over goodwill.

In a healthy church, caring members coordinate their activities to fulfill the mission of Christ. In an unhealthy church, codependent members direct their energy to propping up the self-esteem of insecure leaders. My prayer is that you will identify with a sound congregation dedicated to helping you and your loved ones reach your spiritual potential.

Having said that, no congregation is perfect, so we must commit ourselves to helping one another improve. This will require three things:

(1) **Mindfulness:** None of us is infinitely capable, so we must look out for one another.

(2) **Acceptance:** We all have faults, so we must get better at forgiving than judging.

(3) **Encouragement:** Everyone battles self-doubt, so we must dispense more courage than criticism.

Churches are human soil for spiritual growth. Every congregation has problems, but some have a never-ending pattern of upheaval. Thank God for elders who create a healthy atmosphere to help us succeed in our collective mission and personal goals.

How can you tell if your church environment is right for you and your family? You will feel more challenged than anxious and more excited than oppressed. Leaders will welcome your feedback and encourage honest questions. People will smile more than frown and cheer more than complain.

Truly sound churches honor God's Word by honoring one another. To love you is to honor your worth. To respect you is to honor your dignity. To admonish you is to honor your potential. What winning teams do best is bring out the best in one another. And that raises a final question: What are you contributing to God's team?

Growth Plan No. 1

Area of Growth to work on:

_____

**Choose one strategy to implement first
as you try to improve in this area of growth.**

_____

_____

_____

**Name the day, time and place when you
will begin to take action, if possible.**

Day: _____

Time: _____

Place: _____

**List three ways you can make sure you
follow through with your commitment.**

1 _____

2 _____

3 _____

**With whom will you share your growth plan
to get support? When will you do this?**

_____

_____

_____

Ask God to help you glorify Him by growing in this area
(pray now and daily for this goal).

Growth Plan No. 2

Area of Growth to work on:

_____

**Choose one strategy to implement first
as you try to improve in this area of growth.**

_____

_____

_____

**Name the day, time and place when you
will begin to take action, if possible.**

Day: _____

Time: _____

Place: _____

**List three ways you can make sure you
follow through with your commitment.**

1 _____

2 _____

3 _____

**With whom will you share your growth plan
to get support? When will you do this?**

_____

_____

_____

Ask God to help you glorify Him by growing in this area
(pray now and daily for this goal).

Growth Plan No. 3

Area of Growth to work on:

_____

**Choose one strategy to implement first
as you try to improve in this area of growth.**

_____

_____

_____

**Name the day, time and place when you
will begin to take action, if possible.**

Day: _____

Time: _____

Place: _____

**List three ways you can make sure you
follow through with your commitment.**

1 _____

2 _____

3 _____

**With whom will you share your growth plan
to get support? When will you do this?**

_____

_____

_____

Ask God to help you glorify Him by growing in this area
(pray now and daily for this goal).

Answers to Chapter Questions

Chapter 1

1. Stories (parables).
2. Sowing, fishing, shepherding, etc.
3. Face them, rather than hide from them.
4. To teach players valuable lessons about the game of life.
5. God.
6. Church.
7. Bible.
8. Growth (abundant life).
9. Satan.
10. Faithfulness, functionality, fruitfulness, fulfillment and fearlessness.

Chapter 2

1. He sees far into your future and deep into your heart.
2. His ears are open to your prayers, and His heart is open to your cares.
3. He knows the wiles of the devil and is not susceptible to his trick plays.
4. He redeems and transforms you while overseeing the universe.
5. He does not fear what Satan or man can do because He is infinite and eternal.
6. He knows your name, personality, strengths and weaknesses.
7. He is credible, reliable and inspirational.
8. He stresses spiritual instruction and continual learning.
9. He never stops challenging you to be your best.
10. He comforts you in your troubles so you can comfort others.

Chapter 3

1. Momentary peace and pleasure.
2. You agree to do something, undertake what you promised, and see it through.
3. It is a pledge backed up by your personal honor.
4. Momentary relief comes at the expense of character and credibility.
5. A dog returning to its vomit.
6. God's devotion to His people.
7. His genuine concern for His followers and the reliable care He provides them.
8. Hear, believe, repent, confess and be baptized.
9. Courage.
10. The Bible: It defines, depicts and demands courage.

Chapter 4

1. An abundance of love.
2. When pride and selfishness enter the picture.
3. One another's contributions.
4. Others' interests, not just their own.
5. A vain person whose egotism disrupts the group.
6. A small group of thoughtful, committed people.
7. Connection, protection and direction.
8. Commitment to elders, to assemblies and to one another.
9. They genuinely care for you, and they are considering multiple viewpoints.
10. Material, emotional and spiritual needs.

Chapter 5

1. Commitment to Christ.
2. Commitment to the body of the church.
3. Commitment to the Word of Christ.
4. It will provide you with tools and perspective to handle whatever comes your way.
5. Your game plan.
6. A why, a when and a where.
7. It is commanded; it is true; it saves; it works.
8. It tells your family you love God and His Word.
9. The parable of the sower (thorny ground).
10. Simplify their lives, and prioritize their schedules.

Chapter 6

1. Why people do not avail themselves of the power of prayer.
2. Through commands, stories, examples and promises.
3. It should be offered to the Father though the Son.
4. Talking to God.
5. He cares about me, He can help me, and I want to please Him.
6. "Not as I will, but as You will."
7. Maturity.
8. Unbelief.
9. Adoration, confession, thanksgiving and supplication.
10. Improvements.

Chapter 7

1. It is the quality that guarantees all the others.
2. Ungodliness and unhappiness.
3. Loss of self-control.

4. Taking responsibility for people and events beyond your control.
5. Making requests.
6. Coaching.
7. Retake control of one small area of your life.
8. Rest, exercise and nutrition.
9. Your mouth, money and moods.
10. Demonstrations of love.

Chapter 8
1. Virtue, service, giving, evangelism and perseverance.
2. The ability to get along with other people.
3. Think like the Spirit.
4. Self-control.
5. By failing to study, pray, worship and fellowship.
6. It involves a continual struggle to exercise self-control.
7. Indwells, intercedes and instructs.
8. It means to bring your life in line with the teaching of the Bible.
9. Dependence on Christ.
10. It refers to the virtues that result from the Spirit's influence on your life.

Chapter 9
1. We need to relearn how to respect ourselves and treat others.
2. To serve.
3. The treatment He received.
4. They walked away.
5. Your growth as a servant.
6. Human needs.
7. Lay up treasure in heaven.
8. By putting others above yourself.
9. Serving others improves you.
10. On hearts.

Chapter 10
1. You reinforce your values and prepare yourself to live within your means.
2. The more affluent one is, the less he gives in proportion to his total income.
3. Faith and love.
4. When the collection plate passes.
5. Your reward will be great.
6. Because it limits what you can receive from the Lord.

7. Spiritual maturity and stability.
8. An average life.
9. The desire to give only grows stronger.
10. Spontaneous acts of charity.

Chapter 11
1. Evangelism.
2. Jesus purchased the church with His blood.
3. Knowledge and confidence to engage others in conversation.
4. You will say less.
5. A life of self-discipline.
6. The fruit of the Spirit.
7. The genuine concern for others that motivates people to share their faith.
8. Your heart is not in heaven, so you will have a hard time convincing others to go there.
9. Persistence.
10. Someone cared enough to invite them.

Chapter 12
1. They did not quit.
2. Be steadfast, be immovable, and abound in the work of the Lord.
3. Persistence (perseverance).
4. In developing a consistent loving nature.
5. Study, fellowship, communion and prayer.
6. To hold your ground.
7. The attitudes and actions of a loving mindset.
8. Refusing to give in to unloving emotions that inflict harm on others.
9. Abounding (full to overflowing).
10. Loving and serving others.

Chapter 13
1. Eternity.
2. Long for heaven.
3. Longing.
4. Fix or concentrate.
5. Christ, God and glory.
6. Reminding them about heaven.
7. Thoughts of heaven.
8. Physical or verbal abuse.
9. Believing God's promises about heaven.
10. He constantly talked about it.